DIOCLETIAN'S PALACE, SPLIT:

RESIDENCE OF A RETIRED ROMAN EMPEROR

DIOCLETIAN'S PALACE, SPLIT:

RESIDENCE OF A RETIRED ROMAN EMPEROR

by

J.J. Wilkes

Professor of the Archaeology of the Roman Provinces
Institute of Archaeology, University of London

© J.J. Wilkes

Publisher: Ian Sanders Memorial Committee

First published in the United Kingdom in 1986 by
The Department of Ancient History and Classical Archaeology,
University of Sheffield, Sheffield S10 2TN

Reprinted with corrections 1986, 1993.

*A cataloguing in publication record for this book
is available from the British Library*

ISBN 0 9521073 0 9

Copies of this volume can be obtained from:

Oxbow Books
Park End Place
Oxford OX1 1HN
England

Printed in Great Britain by

Short Run Press Ltd.
Exeter

CONTENTS

FIGURES

PLATES

PREFACE

This essay is an expanded and updated version of the Second Ian Sanders Memorial Lecture in Classical Archaeology delivered in the University of Sheffield on 2 November 1982. It is a pleasure to recall the warm hospitality of that occasion, notably from Professors Derek Mosely and Keith Branigan and their colleagues.

Diocletian's Palace, though a well-known survival of ancient architecture and far from neglected, tends to be accorded only summary treatment in general works, while the comprehensive accounts compiled before the First World war by Niemann and Hébrard-Zeiller are often not to be found even in specialist libraries. The excellent book on Split by Bulić and Karaman published nearly sixty years ago is also a rarity and has been rendered obsolete by post-war investigation. It is hoped that this brief account will offer a helpful guide to the present state of knowledge of a unique residence about which there is so much yet to be learned.

Inevitably, much of this account is based on the labours of others. Since I first visited Split in 1960 I have derived benefit from the expertise of several Yugoslav colleagues, notably Jerko and Tomislav Marasović, foremost authorities on the remains. From 1968 to 1971 I was privileged to participate in the joint American-Yugoslav excavations under the direction of Professor Sheila McNally of the University of Minnesota. To these and many others I owe a great debt for opportunities to study the remains at first hand during my visits to Dalmatia.

Dr. Susan Walker of the British Museum and Dr. Roger Wilson of Trinity College Dublin read a draft of the text. Both preserved me from error in several matters, though I remain entirely responsible not only for the errors of fact which remain but for opinions which may be unpalatable to some.

The occasion of a reprinting has permitted removal of misprints but no major revision of the text has been attempted. I am grateful to my London colleague Mrs. Judith Higgens for help with this revision. In the matter of production I am grateful to the Ian Sanders Memorial Committee at the University of Sheffield — Dr. John Drinkwater, Dr. Paul Halstead, Dr. John Moreland and Mrs. Barbara Hickman. An addendum on recent publications relating to the Palace appears on p. 127. The text of this edition was prepared by Russell Adams — J.R. Collis Publications, Sheffield.

J.J.W.
February 1993

CHAPTER 1

DIOCLETIAN AND THE TETRARCHY [1]

A CELEBRATION

On the 20th November in the year 303 of our era the city of Rome witnessed yet another imperial celebration, when the victories of the Roman armies were extolled through the traditional triumphal procession and dedicated to the gods. It was to be the last such celebration that the people of Rome would behold. Its centre-piece was victory over the Persians, where images of the defeated enemy in their gorgeous robes recalled the great success over Narses in 298 avenging the humiliating capture of the emperor Valerian nearly forty years before. During the festivities the populace was entertained by shows in the arena and chariot racing in the circus.

The celebrations had been timed to mark also the beginning of the twentieth year (*vicennalia*) of Diocletian's reign. He shared the triumph with his colleague Maximian, whom he had appointed Augustus in 286. In addition to the great success against Persia the two Augusti could take pride from military victories in Britain, Africa, Egypt and along the Rhine and Danube.[2] By these they had revived the military fortunes of the empire. Some had been achieved by the two Caesars, younger army officers appointed on the 1st April 293 to assist the Augusti, Constantius for Maximian in the West and Galerius for Diocletian in the East. The celebration encompassed their tenth year of rule (*decennalia*) which had commenced in the spring of that year.

As the senior Augustus viewed, for the first time it appears, the famous buildings, including his own vast baths, and monuments of the imperial capital, he could reflect with satisfaction that he was the first to attain this anniversary since the good Marcus Aurelius[3] in the second century. Before his own accession in 284 the empire had been shaken to the point of disintegration by invasion, military defeat and civil war, all compounded with a financial chaos. Recovery began with Aurelian (270–5) and continued under Probus and Carus, career officers from humble origins in the Danube provinces.

EMPERORS FROM THE DANUBE LANDS

Diocletian came from Dalmatia, a Latin-speaking Illyrian province along the east shore of the Adriatic. He was born on 22nd December in 243, 244 or 245, but little is known of his origins.[4]

By the age of forty, C. Valerius Diocles (as he was styled before his accession) commanded the imperial mounted bodyguard under Carus during his successful expedition against Persia in 283.[5] Like the emperor he was among a group of senior officers of Danubian origins who had been trained and promoted by Aurelian, the first and one of the greatest Illyrian 'soldier-emperors'.[6] When Carus was killed on campaign in Persia, and his young heir Numerianus discovered dead during the return journey, Diocletian was elected by the army council. On the 20th November 284 he was acclaimed by the troops at Nicomedia in north-west Asia Minor and removed his rival, the praetorian prefect Lucius Aper, by summary execution. In the following spring Diocletian faced Carinus, elder son of Carus, in battle at Margum (Orašje at the mouth of the Morava) near the Danube east of Belgrade. The news of Carinus' death caused all the troops to accept Diocletian as emperor, though in fact he had been worsted in the battle.

Diocletian is to be reckoned among the Illyrian rulers, though his Dalmatian origins were far from the heartland of Illyricum around Sirmium (Mitrovica on the Sava), the strategic crossroads of the Danube provinces. Several rulers, including his fellow Augustus Maximian, came from that area. His own Caesar Galerius came from 'New Dacia', the area east of Belgrade where Aurelian had settled south of the Danube the garrison and civilian population from the abandoned Dacia (Transylvania).[7] The family of Constantius, who was born not later than *c*. 250, apparently originated from the part of Moesia Superior or Inferior which later formed Dacia Ripensis. His son Constantine was born at Naissus (Niš), which lay further south and outside Aurelian's New Dacia.[8]

THE COLLEGE OF FOUR

On the 21st July 285 Diocletian appointed an old army colleague, Maximian, as Caesar and the implication of adoption seemed to assure the succession.[9] In Gaul the state of affairs had become desperate and Maximian, promoted Augustus on 1st April 286, was confronted with provinces suffering from the effects of invasion and rural unrest. The sustained loyalty of this old colleague, stemming from their joint service under Aurelian and Probus, was crucial to Diocletian's success – countering the weakness of a single emperor and the recurring uncertainty over the succession.

When the Augusti met in Milan during the winter of 290–1 they could reflect on military success, marred only by the usurper Carausius in Britain, and a steady improvement in the fortunes of the Empire. Celebration of their achievement could proclaim their concord as a divine gift. Diocletian was the Jupiter figure (*Jovius*), his fellow Augustus the mighty Hercules (*Herculius*) who performed heroic labours against the evils on earth. Their power came from the gods, not from any advertised link with a deified predecessor.[10]

The appointment of two younger army officers as Caesars on 1st March 293 now eliminated all speculation regarding the succession. Coins proclaimed their adoption into the divine houses of Jove and Hercules. As Constantius was invested at Milan and Galerius at Sirmium the college of four emperors – the Tetrarchy – had already been strengthened by a marriage alliance between each Caesar and his Augustus, Constantius to Maximian's Theodora and Galerius to Diocletian's Valeria.[11] Neither union bore fruit and it was in the event to be the sons by earlier marriages of Constantius (Constantine) and Maximian (Maxentius) who would destroy the scheme of a planned succession.

The four ruled as a college for twelve years: laws and public pronouncements were made on their collective behalf, though the position of Diocletian as the senior Augustus was acknowledged:

'Illyricum was the homeland of all of them. For all their lack of culture, their upbringing in the hardships of the country and military lives proved to be the best possible for the state. Whereas it is common knowledge that upright and learned men become more ready to perceive faults, those with an experience of life's hardships, while judging everyone by their merit, pay less attention to such things. And they look up to Valerius (Diocletianus) as a father, as one would to a mighty god. But the harmony of these men was proof that their natural ability and use of sound military experience, such as they had acquired under the command of Aurelian and Probus, almost made up for their lack of noble character' (Aurelius Victor, *De Caes.* 29, 26–9)

3

DEFENCE OF THE FRONTIERS

The military success of the Tetrarchy was consolidated by a systematic strengthening of imperial defences. New fortifications were erected along the frontiers, especially the Rhine, Danube and Euphrates, and many cities were protected with new defensive walls.[12] Some of these will have been projects devised under Probus and Aurelian but the overall impression from the literary and archaeological record is of a major programme of military construction sustained throughout the period. The essential features of the new fortifications were high walls, and projecting towers at the gates, corners and along the perimeter and narrow entrances. All these would assure safety at least for those within. If the appearance alone did not repel the attackers artillery in the towers would soon prove a further deterrent.

In Britain the forts along Hadrian's Wall, some evidently partly derelict, were put back into working order.[13] The defences of Gaul were completed, city walls finished and new forts added to the Rhine frontier. New forts were constructed in the Danube provinces, some named Jovia or Herculia.[14] Here inscriptions from several places along the river proclaim the achievements of the régime in fulsome language, very different from that of earlier times. A recently discovered text from a small fortress just east of the Danube gorge, not far from the site of Trajan's bridge, conveys the message of recovery and security broadcast throughout the empire:

> 'The emperors and Caesars Gaius Valerius Aurelius Diocletianus and Marcus Aurelius Valerius Maximianus, dutiful and blessed invincible Augusti, and Flavius Valerius Constantius and Galerius Valerius Maximianus most noble Caesars, great conquerors of Germans, great conquerors of Samatians, for the everlasting future of the Republic have established this military 'strongpoint.[15]

THE NEW EMPIRE

Though remains of fortifications and buildings convey something of the successes of Diocletian and his colleagues, they are merely a reflection of the profound changes effected in the organisation and the governing of the Empire.[16] Each emperor travelled with a large retinue of officials and a force of household cavalry. The old provinces were subdivided, some into two, three or four, to make new provinces of roughly standard site. These were grouped into twelve dioceses supervised by deputies of the praetorian prefect, who was now in effect the prime minister of each emperor.

4

Provincial governors were relieved of military command. The strength of the army was increased and conscription introduced for the sons of veterans and the rural population as a whole. The frontier troops were increased, and commanded by officers charged with responsibility for specific sections of the frontier. The forces that accompanied the emperors served as the nucleus of a mobile reserve, a field army already formed on several occasions during the emergencies of the third century.

The currency was reformed and a more flexible system of taxation, in cash and in kind, was introduced. By a formula of assessment land was graded according to quality and produce. The needs of the state were levied by an 'indiction' of the level of tax per unit of assessment. Some of the reforms may have caused a crisis that caused the emperor to issue his famous Edict on Maximum Prices in AD 301 (listing charges for goods, services and wages in minute detail). In the preamble a furious Diocletian berates those who would profiteer from the basic needs of fellow citizens. Soon it could not be enforced, as goods were driven off the market.[17]

Diocletian's reforms increased the burdens of empire on all citizens. For all his obvious prejudice there is truth in the analysis of Lactantius, an African Christian appointed by Diocletian professor of Latin Literature at Nicomedia. His later memoir on the deaths of the persecutors is the nearest thing we have to a contemporary account of Diocletian's reign.

'He appointed three men to share his rule, dividing the world into four parts and multiplying the armies, since each of the four strove to have a far larger number of troops than previous emperors had had when they were governing the state alone. The number of recipients began to exceed the number of contributors by so much that, with farmers' resources exhausted by the enormous size of the requisitions, fields became deserted and cultivated land was turned into forest. To ensure that terror was universal, provinces too were cut into fragments; many governors and even more officials were imposed on individual regions, almost on individual cities, and to these were added numerous accountants, controllers and prefects' deputies. The activities of all these people were very rarely civil; they engaged only in repeated condemnations and confiscations, and in exacting endless resources – and the exactions were not just frequent, they were incessant, and involved insupportable injustices. And how could the arrangements for raising soldiers be endured?'

'This same Diocletian with his insatiable greed was never willing that his treasuries should be depleted; he was always amassing surplus wealth and funds for largesse so that he could keep what he was storing complete and inviolate. Since too by his various misdeeds he was causing an immense rise in prices, he tried to fix by law the price of goods put up for sale. Much blood was

5

then shed over small and cheap items, in the general alarm nothing appeared for sale, and the rise in prices got much worse until, after many had met their deaths, sheer necessity led to the repeal of the law.'

'In addition Diocletian had a limitless passion for building, which led to an equally limitless scouring of the provinces to raise workers, craftsmen, wagons, and whatever is necessary for building operations. Here he built basilicas, there a circus, a mint, an arms-factory, here he built a house for his wife, there one for his daughter. Suddenly a great part of the city (Nicomedia) was destroyed, and all the inhabitants started to migrate with their wives and children, as if the city had been captured by the enemy. And when these buildings had been completed and the provinces ruined in the process – he would say: "They have not been built rightly; they must be done in another way. They then had to be pulled down and altered – perhaps only to come down a second time." '[18]

Between the two Augusti the polemicist offers a comparison which, for all its hostility, is nonetheless instructive: 'Diocletian was greedier but more hesitant, whereas Maximian was less greedy but bolder.'[19]

A NEW IMAGE

The courts of the Tetrarchy afforded no scope for the colourful anecdotes of a Suetonius, the bleak analysis of a Tacitus or the dinner-party gossip of a Younger Pliny. That Diocletian remains a remote and almost invisible figure, when compared with many of his predecessors, is not merely due to the absence of such writers but also the consequence of the profound change, deliberately contrived, in the image of the ruler conveyed to his subjects.[20]

Surrounded by their entourage of the enlarged imperial administration, the emperors lived and worked in seclusion remote from the gaze of their subjects. Access was controlled by a corps of personal attendants. Though often moving from one part of their domain to another, the emperors built palaces at those places where they now tended to remain for long periods. Whereas earlier rulers when not in Rome travelled from city to city and resided often in the private houses of leading citizens, the Tetrarchs governed from such cities as Trier, Milan, Sirmium, Nicomedia and Antioch. These became imperial capitals in the sense that large palaces were erected for the emperors and their courts. Through the adoption of ornate robes and a rigid ceremonial, modelled on the Persian court, the emperor became a remote figure, inspiring awe in his subjects on the rare occasions he appeared before them.

Plate 1   Heads of two Venice Tetrarchs

Until the middle of the third century the portraits of Roman emperors had followed a tradition that went back to Alexander the Great. The idealised though recognisable features of the ruler were often portrayed with an upward gaze, seeking — as was their due — inspiration from the gods. Such portraits of emperors from Augustus to Gallienus are a familiar component in collections of sculpture from all over the Empire.[21]

The Tetrarchs suppressed the personal identity for a collective image that none could fail to recognise. The eyes stare out from features lined and drawn from the huge burdens of rule. The flowing locks of hair and philosopher's beard now give way to the close-cropped hair and beard upon a 'cubist' head. No upward look towards the gods; theirs was an inborn quality of divinity, the gift of destiny, as they laboured under protection of Jupiter and Hercules.[22] One expression of this is the Venice Tetrarchs, two pairs of porphyry figures shown in fraternal embrace, once in Constantinople and now built into the corner of St Mark's in Venice (Plate 1). As has been observed: 'The individual has disappeared in the creation of a type which has meaning in a new hierarchical order for mankind'.[23] The new imperial image, which was to prevail throughout much of the fourth

7

century, casts into confusion modern attempts to identify with this or that ruler the Tetrarchic heads which survive, as the sculptor was constrained to represent the office and not the man.

THE ATTACK ON CHRISTIANITY

Diocletian was to rule for eighteen months after his *vicennalia* celebration in Rome. A serious and prolonged illness in the autumn and winter of 304 brought a decision, possibly sudden and unpremeditated, to abdicate, which was carried through at Nicomedia on the 1st May 305 before a large parade of troops. The last two years of his reign witnessed the Great Persecution, the last imperial onslaught on the followers of Christ. His illness may have appeared an act of vengeance by the Christian God. Nor can one discount the influence of his wife Prisca and daughter Valeria, whom Lactantius appears to identify as Christians. In retirement Diocletian lived to witness Galerius the arch-persecutor, stricken with the agonies of a fatal disease, issue from Serdica an edict of toleration on the 30th April 311 which included even a request for prayers on his behalf.[24]

The Danubian emperors, from humble origins and with limited education rose to power through years of military service. Very different from their urbane and cynical predecessors of the first and second centuries, they exhibited a simple and genuine belief in the old gods and ideals of Rome. Diocletian deeply resented any semblance of impiety towards his Jupiter. Early in his reign he hounded the followers of Mani, a third-century teacher whose followers were widespread in Egypt and Syria, partly for their hostility to the gods but also on the grounds that they were perceived as a fifth column during the war with Persia.[25]

An attempt to revive worship of the old gods may have served only to reveal how much ground Christianity had gained since the last systematic persecution under Decius in the middle of the third century. Christian writers blamed Galerius, whose mother was 'a worshipper of the gods of the mountains, and a highly superstitious woman'[26], for the edict of the 23rd February 303 which began the Great Persecution, by ordering the burning of scriptures, dismantling of churches and a prohibition on assembly for Christian worship. Diocletian was more cautious. Certainly he had been affronted by acts of defiance on the part of Christians serving in the army, but he appeared to believe that dismissal and loss of privileges were more effective weapons than the execution of martyrs.[27] Before assenting to the persecution he sent a *haruspex* to seek the judgement of the oracle of Apollo at Miletus. This was the famous shrine at Didyma, a few miles south of Miletus, which enjoyed great popularity during the Roman Empire and appears to have had a special attraction for Diocletian. The response was suitably oracular: 'he responded as one would expect from an enemy of the religion of god'. Faced with the alliance of his friends, his Caesar and Apollo, Diocletian gave way and settled for an insistence on caution.[28]

On the first day a party of soldiers demolished the Christian building in Nicomedia which stood in full view of the Palace. Another edict posted the following day deprived Christians of any rank they held. Reports of disturbances led to a second edict ordering arrest of all clergy. Celebration of the *vicennalia* in November was marked by an amnesty. The gaols were now full and the authorities insisted on the sacrifice test by a third edict before internees were to be set free. A fourth edict early in 304 required everyone to perform sacrifice. The persecution was carried through with gusto in the east but was more haphazard in the west. Many were tortured and imprisoned, though the number killed was small, the death penalty being reserved for deliberate acts of defiance.

ILLNESS AND ABDICATION

The *vicennalia* of the Augusti and the *decennalia* of the Caesars were commemorated by a triumphal arch and a monument near the *rostra* in the Roman forum, where statues of the Tetrarchs were placed on columns and that of Jupiter on a fifth, higher than the rest.[29]

Diocletian left Rome on the 20th December, distressed, it was reported, by the disrespectful and rowdy behaviour of the populace. Instead he entered on his ninth consulship on the 1st January at Ravenna. He spent much of the next year on the Danube frontier but had reached Nicomedia by the end of August. During the journey he was dogged by an illness. He managed to conclude his *vicennalia* on 20th November by inaugurating a new circus but his failing health was plain for all to see.[30]

During the winter rumours of his death were spreading – deliberately concealed it was alleged until Galerius should arrive – but a public appearance on the 1st March revealed not a restored Augustus but one scarcely recognisable through the wasting effects of a long illness. On the 1st May 305, before a great parade of troops on a hill a few miles outside Nicomedia, he laid aside his imperial robe. He was weak and tired and sought rest after years of labour. He was handing over power to men of proven ability who were more robust. He commended Galerius Augustus to the troops and personally invested the new Caesar Maximin Daia, a relative of Galerius, with his own purple. 'Once again he became Diocles. Then descending from the platform the retiring emperor was conveyed through the city in a carriage and despatched to his native country.[31]' At Milan on the same day Maximian resigned his power to Constantius and invested the new Caesar Severus before retiring to his estate in Campania.[32]

A Christian version made Galerius force Diocletian into retirement but it must be doubted whether Lactantius, though an eye-witness of the event, was really party to the secrets of the Palace. It seems highly likely that illness and exhaustion decided the timing though it is reasonable to regard simultaneous abdication of the Augusti in favour of their Caesars as the intended fulfilment of the Tetrarchy. The action was unprecedented and was never imitated.[33] The voluntary withdrawal of an emperor to the status of private citizen – though he retained the dignity of an Augustus – caused universal amazement. Perhaps the true cause is revealed in the comment of a fourth-century historian, that Diocletian cared nothing for personal ambition.[34] He was probably then in his early sixties and may have survived for another ten years.

THE RETIRED AUGUSTUS

Perhaps Diocletian, whose habit was to contemplate the future course of events,[35] may have foreseen that his Tetrarchy would fail its crucial test – transmission of power. Yet it is unlikely that even he could have anticipated that it would be destroyed so quickly by the traditional assertion of hereditary succession.[36] In the following year the army in Britain acclaimed Constantine, following the death of his father Constantius, the senior Augustus. In Italy the unpopular Severus was deposed after Maxentius had persuaded his father Maximian to forsake his reluctant retirement. Galerius invaded Italy but found himself confronted by an understanding between Maximian and the latter's son-in-law, Constantine. Maximian was driven by his son Maxentius back into retirement but the latter then faced a usurper in Africa. Baffled by what seemed a return to the worst years of Gallienus half a century before, Galerius persuaded Diocletian to leave his retirement home on the Adriatic and attend a reunion of the surviving Tetrarchs at Carnuntum on the Danube in November 308.[37]

Diocletian rebuffed the suggestion of Maximian that he should return to power not by upbraiding his old colleague for his foolish conduct but by the response that he would never have asked the question if he could see the cabbages grown with his own hands in retirement.[38] Maximian was forced into retirement for a second time, his son Maxentius was deemed an usurper and replaced by a new Augustus, Licinius, colleague of Galerius and a compatriot from Dacia Ripensis. The final collapse of the Tetrarchy was marked by the promotion to Augustus of the Caesars Constantine and Maximin who had taken offence at the rank of Licinius. In the event Diocletian was destined to outlive the other Tetrarchs. Maximian, the old Augustus who had found refuge with Constantine, made yet another bid for power at Arles and was forced to suicide in the summer of 310. Less than a year later Galerius perished in agony.

Such was the seclusion of Diocletian's retirement that neither the date nor the manner of his death is known for certain. His last years were clouded by the misfortunes of his own family. After the death of Galerius, his widow and Diocletian's daughter Valeria Augusta moved to the court of Maximin Daia, to whom they had been commended by Galerius. When she rebuffed his politically motivated proposal of marriage – 'while the ashes of her husband were still warm' – Valeria and her mother Prisca were banished from Nicomedia to Syria. From this solitude they succeeded in sending a message to Diocletian; his first request to Licinius that his daughter be permitted to return to her father was refused and even when he sent 'a relation of his own, a military man of authority, to remind Maximin of the benefits he had received from Diocletian and to beg for her return, he too came back with his mission uncompleted, reporting that his entreaties had been fruitless'.[39] If, as seems likely, Diocletian's death preceded that of Maximin in the summer of 313, then he was spared the sight of his wife and daughter falling victim (*c.* September 314) to the cruel vengeance of Licinius who hunted down the families of Galerius and his nephew Maximin.[40]

Lactantius's account of Diocletian's death, which may have occurred on 3rd December 311,[41] is linked with Constantine's attack on the memory of Maximian:

'At the same time (as Maximin's refusal to permit Valeria and Prisca to join Diocletian) statues of the elder Maximian were being torn down on the orders of Constantine, and any pictures in which he had been portrayed were being removed. And because the two old men had usually been painted together, this meant that the pictures of both were being taken down at the same time. Diocletian thus saw happening to him in his own lifetime what had never happened to an emperor before; and afflicted with this double grief, he took the decision that he should die. He would throw himself this way and that, his soul in a torment of grief, taking neither sleep nor food. He sighed and groaned, he frequently wept. He was for ever twisting and turning his body, now on his bed, now on the ground. So this emperor who for twenty years had been most fortunate, was cast down by God to a life of humiliation, smitten with injuries which led him to hate life itself, and finally extinguished by starvation and grief.'

CHAPTER 2

RESIDENCE FOR A RETIRED AUGUSTUS

THE *PATRIA* OF DIOCLETIAN

Diocletian's destination when he left Nicomedia after his abdication on 1st May 305 was a residence at the water's edge on the Dalmatian coast, the land of his birth more than sixty years before. The Roman province of Dalmatia comprised not only the Adriatic coast which bears that name today, but a large triangle of territory, mainly mountainous and tree-covered, reaching inland almost to Belgrade at the confluence of the rivers Sava and Danube. Conquest of this area was the principal military achievement of Augustus' principate.[42]

The coast and islands had attracted Greek colonists as early as the fifth century BC. By the early second century BC, as the Romans achieved dominance in the area, settlers came from Italy to settle along the coast with its mild climate and many harbours. Navigation routes up and down the Adriatic tended to follow the Dalmatian rather than the Italian shore. Away from the coast, the interior held little attraction for settlers and the native peoples were slow to adapt to the Roman way of life. The land had two principal assets, rich deposits of minerals (silver-bearing lead, iron ore and some gold) and a hardy population well suited for military service. Both were exploited by the Romans from the first century AD onwards. Salonae, later Salona, was in origin a settlement of the native Delmatae, seized by the Romans and made a colony of settlers by Julius Caesar (*colonia Martia Julia Salonae*).[43] Soon Salona became the principal city of the province, the starting-point of major routes inland and the residence of the consular imperial legates who governed Dalmatia until the middle of the third century.[44] Diocletian's residence lay within the fertile territory of Caesar's colony (Figure 2). This had been surveyed and divided by a grid of roads and tracks into blocks of land 776 yards square, or *centuriae* of 20 by 20 *actus*.[45] These served to register the ownership and tax liability of the colony's land. Aerial photography has revealed, through surviving boundaries and tracks, that the system enclosed not only all the surrounding mainland but was also continued to some of the islands.

In Dalmatia Roman settlers and the natives remained apart until the late first century. Under the Flavians Roman citizenship and city institutions began to spread among the native peoples but on a limited scale. It was never one of the 'dynamic regions' of the Roman world, Cisalpina (Po Valley), Narbonensis (Provence and Languedoc) and Baetica (Andalusia), whence came emperors and senators from a native and settler background.[46] It was the veteran colony of Aequum (near Sinj twenty miles inland from Salona), settled under Claudius (AD 41–54), which produced the most distinguished figures recorded from Dalmatia, Sex. Julius Severus, who was consul in AD 127 and Hadrian's best general, and his son, or kinsman, Cn. Julius Verus, a general under Pius and Marcus.[47] The origins of Diocletian are not, like those of Septimius Severus at Lepcis Magna,[48] to be sought in the municipal families of an earlier generation. He emerged evidently from the large servile and freedmen population, which inscriptions record at Salona during the Principate.[49] The ancestors of Valerius Diocles may have been native Dalmatians enslaved in the early Principate. It may well be that Diocletian's origins in a great flourishing city such as Salona contributed to his unique talent for civil and military administration, to be compared favourably with the out and out military qualities of his fellow Illyrians from Pannonia and Moesia.[50]

ASPALATHOS

There is scope for much speculation regarding the siting of the residence, since we know nothing of precisely how or when it was created. We may assume perhaps that sufficient had been completed to house Diocles when his ship appeared offshore sometime in May 305. As one passes the larger Dalmatian islands, Black Corcyra (Korčula) Pharos (Hvar) and Brattia (Brač), the mountains of the mainland loom ever larger, the sheer face of Kozjak (677m) and the mass of Mosor (1330m). On a saddle between these stands the fortress of Klis, where even long before the military road was built by the Romans, traffic had passed between the Adriatic coast (primorje) and the interior (zagora).[51] Below the grey cliffs of Kozjak a strip of fertile land, green with vines, figs and olives, encloses the great bay. At its east corner, near the mouth of the river Jadro which emerges in full flow from the spur of

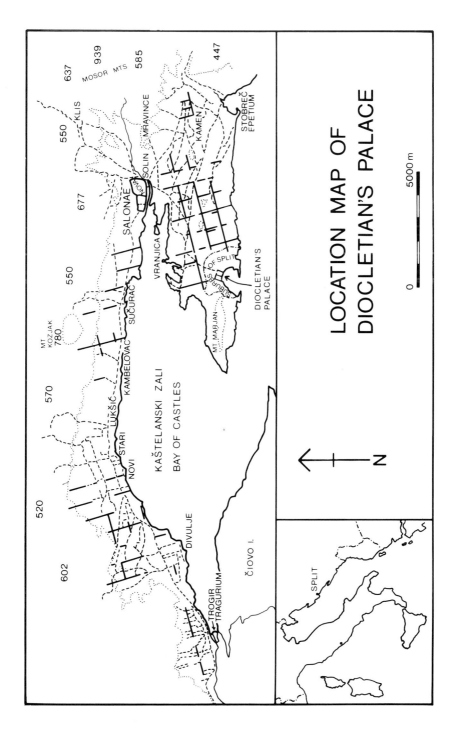

Figure 1   Location map of Salona and Split.

Mosor, lie the remains of Salona. Along the north shore of the bay are seven castles built by local people in the fifteenth century following the Turkish conquest of Bosnia, and which give the bay its modern name, Bay of Castles (Kaštelanski Zaljev).[52] On the west the bay is closed off by the island Čiovo (ancient Bua or Boa), where the small town of Trogir (ancient Tragurium) is set astride the narrow channel between island and mainland. On the south and east the Bay of Castles is closed off by a peninsula which ends in the wooded hill of Marijan (178m), in antiquity the site of a shrine to the goddess Diana.[53] Between the Marijan and the small harbour of Stobreč (the ancient Epetium) the land slopes gently to the sea, ending in low cliffs divided by several small sheltered inlets. The emperor's residence was situated near the centre of one of these three bays, facing the islands of Šolta (ancient Solentia) and Brač (Brattia), with Hvar (Pharos) just visible beyond the latter.

Before the arrival of the Romans the commerce of the area was controlled by the Greek colonies on the larger islands, the Parians at Pharos (Starigrad) and Syracusan Issa (Vis) on the islands of the same names. Several other Greek settlements are known to have existed along this part of the Dalmatian coast but none compared with Pharos or Issa. The latter enjoyed a Roman alliance in the third century BC, had made a settlement on the island of Black Corcyra (Lumbarda, on Korčula), and later claimed protection for her outposts on the mainland at Tragurium (Trogir) and Epetium (Strobreč). The question as to whether Salona was also settled by Greeks, Issaeans or others, remains unresolved.[54]

The earliest record of Diocletian's residence may be on the Peutinger Map *(Tabula Peutingeriana)* named after Konrad Peutinger who acquired it in 1508.[55] When complete it was a road map of the world from Britain to India and from Germany to Africa compressed into a narrow strip 6.82m long and 0.34m wide. Its origin has been the subject of debate but a current view is that it was based on the routes of the Imperial Post *(cursus publicus)*. The symbols, of which there are seven basic types, indicate not the relative status of the place but the sort of facilities available. It is believed that the map was compiled originally in the third century, then revised in the eastern empire in the reign of Theodosius II (AD 408–450). Its present version dates from the thirteenth century.

The map records the route along the Dalmatian coast and from Salona two major routes to the Sava valley, one to Servitium, the other via the Drina valley to Sirmium. *Epetium* (Stobreč) is marked as the next point on the coast road after Salona, only four Roman miles away. From Epetium a branch road runs along the coast to Spalato *(Spalatum)* after four miles and then to *Ad Dianam* at the tip of the Marijan peninsula. A direct route leads from Spalatum to Salona, a four-mile stretch, which joins the Epetium road before the Jadro crossing. No symbol is indicated for the site of the residence.

Spalatum appears to have been the Latin version of Aspalathos, which was evidently the original name of the place. The *Notitia Dignitatum* (Register of Offices) compiled at the end of the fourth or early in the fifth century, lists imperial factories in the eastern half of the empire under the charge of the paymaster general *(comes sacrarum largitionum)*. Among these is an imperial factory at Aspalatum in Dalmatia, the textile factory named 'Jovensis' (after Diocletian Jovius) under its procurator.[56] The Latin form appears twice, as Spalathron or Spalatrum in the Ravenna Cosmography, compiled by an anonymous cleric in the seventh century.[57] In the tenth century Constantine Porphyrogenitus cites the Greek version Aspalathos. He offers the erroneous etymology that the name of the place, founded by Diocletian, derived from *palatium* or palace, and a similar explanation was offered by the thirteenth century Spalato historian Thomas the Archdeacon.[58] As indeed has long been recognized, the name Spalato has nothing to do with *Palatium* or Palace, but derives from the original name of the place, after the Aspalathos shrub, which may date back to the period of Greek exploration and settlement of the area. The Elder Pliny describes Aspalathos as a white thorn which grows to the size of a small tree with a flower similar to a rose. It was used in several ancient recipes for perfumes and could well have been widespread along the Dalmatian coast.[59]

No trace has come to light of any pre-existing structure on the site of the residence. Nevertheless, it is improbable that such a massive construction will not have caused a great disturbance to the area, whether or not it involved the demolition of existing buildings. Most likely there was a small settlement somewhere on or near the bay and the surrounding land will have been intensively cultivated, by small farms along the grid of lanes and tracks of the Salona centuriation. None of the earlier architectural fragments found in the remains (see below n. 139) can be linked with any structure, though foundations of what were thought to have been an earlier building were briefly exposed after a fire near the Mausoleum in 1924; recent excavations, however, have revealed nothing of this.[60] The well-known 'bird's eye view' by E. Hébrard includes a smaller villa on the west of the residence in the belief that only such a pre-existing building could have forced Diocletian's residence away from the ideal place at the centre of the bay towards a site constricted on the east by a natural gulley.[61]

MATERIALS FOR BUILDING: LOCAL LIMESTONE, TUFA AND BRICK

Diocletian's residence offers one of the last surviving examples of the capabilities of the imperial building industry. The talents of local and foreign craftsmen were co-ordinated in a building that matches for its use of local stone and imported marbles even the colossal structures with which a century earlier Septimius Severus had endowed his birthplace, Lepcis Magna in Tripolitania.[62] The great quantity of freshly-quarried limestone used in the construction came from two local quarries, both well-placed for transport by water to the building-site. Most came from quarries near the north coast of the island Brač (Brattia), at Strazišće, Rasohe and Plate, whence it could be shipped for the distance of 20km from the harbour at Splitska, which lies directly opposite Split.[63] Several quarries in the area are worked today and in modern times the stone has been exported to distant lands. It may be that the Brač quarries were imperially owned, even if actually leased for working by local contractors. Such places *(metalla)* are identified as the destination for condemned criminals and doubtless many such perished in servitude on the island.[64] Remains of the ancient workings are still visible. On one face there is a roughly-cut standing figure easily identified as Hercules (Plate 2) — in his form as patron of stone-cutters *(Hercules Saxanus)*.[65] The imperial presence brings the dedication to Hercules Augustus erected by a serving soldier at the Plate quarry, concerned with cutting the column-capitals for the baths of Licinius' residence at Sirmium *(Thermae Licinianae)*. This is likely to have taken place in 308–316, when Licinius was in residence at Sirmium, soon after the presumed completion of Diocletian's residence.[66] Brač stone has a consistently even texture and its quarries are ideally placed for water transport. When worked and polished it has almost the sheen of a marble from the Aegean. It is used throughout the area, and as far into the hinterland as it can be reasonably transported, and elsewhere in the Adriatic, including Venice. The most notable building to display its qualities is the fifteenth century cathedral at Šibenik, on the coast north of Split, with carvings by George the Dalmatian (Juraj Dalmatinac).[67]

The second source of building-stone was the quarry at St Elias (St Ilija or Sutilija), on the mainland near Trogir.[68] The stone is of comparable quality to Brač stone, and acquires over the centuries a cream patina more attractive than the whitish grey of the latter. The Trogir stone was used for the North

Plate 2   Relief of Hercules in quarry on Brač. *Photo: Bulić-Karaman*, pl. 66

Gate and makes a contrast with the Brač stone employed throughout the Peristyle, Mausoleum and Temple, as well as the perimeter walls. In addition to limestone and mortar there was also obtained locally a tufa (sedra) employed in the vaulted ceilings of the basements to the private apartments. It is a porous, light and easily-worked stone obtained from the beds of streams in the limestone karst of Dalmatia, in this instance most likely that of the Jadro.[69] The construction demanded many thousands of bricks, most of a standard size (0.33m square and 30mm thick), in horizontal courses in the walls and for innumerable arches, window — and door-vaults. The dome of the Mausoleum, with bricks set in decorative feather-patterns, was made from bricks of inferior quality, poorly fired from badly prepared clay. These bear the stamp DALMATIA (or DALMATI) and appear to be the products of local kilns specially set up for this project.[70] During preceding centuries bricks of fired clay were imported in large quantities, especially from factories, some imperially owned, in the region of Aquileia at the head of the Adriatic. Their products are found in almost every Roman settlement along the Dalmatian coast and the near hinterland. The roof of the Mausoleum contains many of these imported tiles, evidently removed from older buildings. No less than 537 bore the stamp Q CLODIVS AMBROSIVS, one of the mass-producers at Aquileia, which for a time at least was imperially owned.[71]

IMPORTED MARBLE, MOSAICS AND SCULPTURES

Import of marble, not only of columns, capitals and wall-veneer but also of coffins (sarcophagi), most roughed out and partly finished, is known in Dalmatia from at last as early as the first century AD.[72] With only a meagre knowledge of earlier Roman buildings in Dalmatia, it is hard to judge how extensive this trade was — at least in respect of building material — into Dalmatia. In some areas marble was a desirable and necessary improvement on inferior local stones, but the cost of import will have been less justified with a high-quality local stone which imitated the qualities of marble.[73] The most obvious instance of imported marbles at Split are whole columns, which were removed from existing buildings (perhaps temples in Egypt), and incorporated in the Peristyle and the Mausoleum portico. Among white marbles, one of the commonest is a grey-banded variety from the island of Proconnesos in the Sea of Marmara, not far from Istanbul.[74] There is also Euboean 'cipollino' from Carystos, and a Breccia Corallina, also perhaps from the north Aegean. Evidently an urgent need for finished columns brought not only second-hand marble but a variety of Egyptian granites, red 'imperial' porphyry, red granite from Syene (Assuan), and grey granite from quarries in the eastern desert *(Mons Claudianus)*. In some cases columns did not match precisely the required dimensions and had to be trimmed down for use.[75]

An exception to the overall impression of haste in construction — re-use of ill-fitting columns of different stones — is the supply of marble capitals. Some, notably one from the east–west cross-street, are of Proconnesian marble and have been matched closely with those in the villa at Piazza Armerina in Sicily and at the Palace of Galerius in Thessalonica. It has been asserted, and denied, that these can be grouped apart from capitals being produced by those imperial quarries at the same period.[76] Many interior walls were covered with marble veneer, though none has survived *in situ*. The bath-suites had white marble lining for their plunges. Other chambers had a variety of coloured marbles — whether re-used or freshly quarried is not known — many of which occur in debris from several places within the walls.[77]

Small fragments recorded *in situ* attest that both the Mausoleum and the Vestibule had mosaic decoration on the walls and in their domes.[78] They are likely to have been the work of specialist craftsmen but nothing can be inferred from the remains regarding either their quality or decorative schemes. The floor mosaics, four in the corridors around the court (?*palaestra*) north of the eastern baths, a similar group at the lower level east of the vestibule, and one in the north-east quarter, all have simple geometric patterns.[79] All the mosaics appear to have been laid when the residence was first built. The quality of workmanship is adequate rather than outstanding and the design uninspired, such as one might expect to meet in the average town-house or villa in the area.

The sphinx was a mythical animal of Egypt, with the body of a lion and a human face. In Bronze Age and Classical Greece it appears in female form and figures in several myths. The sphinx's attributes made them especially suitable as the guardian figures of tombs. Perhaps as many as four sphinxes were brought from Egypt, presumably along with the columns.[80] They were placed either side of the steps leading up to the Mausoleum. One, carved from black basalt, 2.46m long, 0.65m wide and 1.00m high, is now between the columns of the Peristyle, a little removed from its original place south of the entrance and facing north rather than west as it would originally have been (Plate 3). The two front limbs are human rather than animal and hold a vessel intended for offerings. Around the plinth are carved a series of bearded and unbearded warriors, roped together at the neck. On the shields borne by each one are engraved the names of Palestinian cities, perhaps added by the conqueror Rameses II (1279–1212 BC) on a sphinx belonging originally to the earlier Pharaoh Tuthmose III (1504–1450 BC).

The other sphinx, smaller and now headless, which may have confronted the first, is made of Assuan granite; it was removed to the Archaeological Museum in 1875. It is 1.51m long, 0.45m wide and 0.44m high to the point where the head is broken away. The inscription is a dedication for Amenhotep III(1386–1349) BC). The head of a sphinx walled up in an old house in the north-west quarter does not belong to that in the Museum. It is of pink granite. The placing of sphinxes around the great Octagon puts beyond doubt its identification as Diocletian's Mausoleum.[81]

No trace has been recorded of the free-standing statues which stood in various locations, notably a group on the plinth above the monumental entrance on the south of the Peristyle and possibly above the flanking colonnades. The four plinths at the North Gate, with dimensions implying a hierarchy, may have been surmounted with porphyry figures of the Tetrarchs

Plate 3   Sphinx in Peristyle.

(see below p.30). There is nothing to indicate what images might have been placed in the four niches in the facade of the North Gate or in the two niches at the East and West Gates.[82]

ARCHITECTS AND BUILDERS

We have no record of any individual official, architect, craftsman or any other who may have been concerned with the building of Diocletian's residence.[83] Nor has any evidence been forthcoming relating to any local organization which will have been created for a major project that must have involved planning and co-ordination of workers and supplies and, one assumes, great expense. In default of literary or epigraphic testimony we can only make inferences from the surviving remains. Something can be deduced from overall plan and character, the nature and variety of ornament, and the techniques of construction. Further, as we shall see later, many theories have been advanced from wide-ranging comparisons of the remains at Split with Roman civil and military architecture of the period. Yet ignorance subsists: all we know for certain is the approximate date and the purpose.

It is hard to determine the significance of the name Zotikos carved, presumably at the time of construction, on the hidden side of a pilaster, on the North Gate. The Greek name — which means 'full of life' — is common in the Roman Empire among slaves and freedmen, and the four attested examples from Salona and its area are persons of this status.[85] Conceivably we have here the name of a local craftsman but the Greek letters point more to a stone-carver from the eastern provinces. The presence of Greek-speaking craftsmen is presumably indicated by the large number of Greek letters carved as 'masons' marks' on many stone blocks throughout the residence. Almost every letter of the alphabet is represented at some point or other. The number and variety of such marks is demonstrated on the recently-exposed inner faces of the perimeter walls and towers, at all levels.[86] The sign of the dolphin, and the Greek letter delta (Δ) and the omicron (O) carved beneath, noted on the inner face of the perimeter wall has prompted the conclusion that some of the workmen were Christians. The known strength of Christianity in Salona and the among the urban lower classes in general at that period makes it more than likely that at least some were indeed Christians. Yet it is far from certain that the symbol and letters were carved as a hidden gesture of defiance towards the pagan beliefs of the person for whom the residence was intended.[87]

CHAPTER 3

THE SURVIVING REMAINS

AREA

Diocletian's residence combined in its enclosing walls the strength of a fortress, in its main streets and sacred precincts the grandeur of a city, and in its private apartments the elegance and luxury of a great villa (Plate 4). That concatenation draws together the three principal forms of Roman architecture that distinguish the era of its famous occupant, the transition from the Principate of Augustus to the late Empire of the fourth and fifth centuries. Its surviving remains (Figure 2), now compacted and truncated after seventeen centuries of medieval Spalato and modern Split, can still offer to a visitor, struggling through its congested streets in the sultry heat of a Dalmatian summer, much of that fascination which has attracted architects and antiquaries since the Classical Revival in the eighteenth century.[88]

The site inclines from north to south more than eight metres to the water's edge, from east to west less than two metres. Overall the area occupied is over 3.8ha (c. 9.5 acres) but is not an exact rectangle, as the external

Plate 4   Model of Diocletian's Palace (Hébrard-Zeiller).

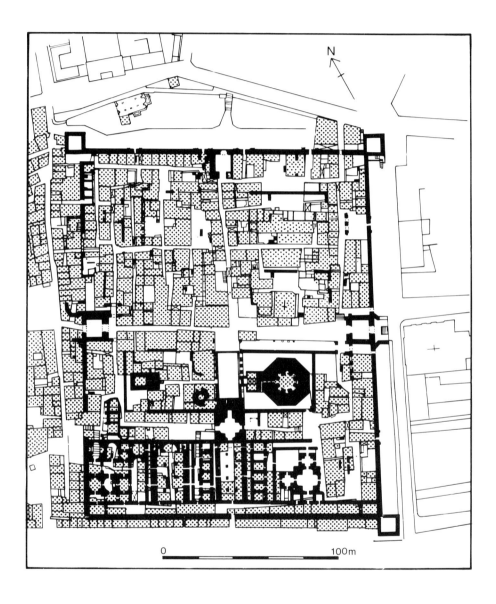

Figure 2   Remains of Diocletian's Palace (1964). Based on Marasović, *Urbs*, p.25.

26

dimensions of the sides indicate, east and west 215.5m, north 175m and south 181m.[89] Internal measurements are 191.25, 151 and 157.5m respectively, an area of nearly 3ha (nearly 7.25 acres). That is about one sixth the area of a legionary fortress of the Principate, devised for a notional strength of 5,400 soldiers and around twice the area of a fort intended for 500 auxiliaries. In 1926, when the houses of medieval and renaissance Spalato were still intact, the population within the walls was 3,200 persons in 278 houses.

WALLS AND TOWERS[90]

The outer face of the perimeter wall was an unadorned surface of smooth-dressed and closely-fitted limestone blocks (Plate 5). The courses are often tapered to the lie of the ground, but average 0.5m in height. The blocks are secured to each other by iron clamps set in lead without the use of mortar. The inner face was similar and between the two lines of facing stones, most of which were 0.40-0.60m thick, a core of rubble set in mortar made up the wall thickness of 2.10m. No bonding courses of brick were employed in the

Plate 5   North wall of palace.

27

perimeter walls, nor was there a plinth or offset above the footings set on the natural rock, which were left roughly finished.

At the upper level the wall narrows to 1.15m thick, two courses below the window apertures of a patrol walkway. These average 2.0m wide and are 3.10 to 3.90m high to the centre of the arches, formed by two rows of tapered stones (outer of 15, inner of 11). A simple S-cornice runs around the entire perimeter, not at the same level but following approximately the slope of natural ground. It is 1.10m higher at the north-east corner than at the west gate, the lowest point where it is still preserved. On the west half of the north wall the cornice is 22m above sea level but in the east half it is 0.82m lower, with an abrupt change in level concealed by the east octagonal tower of the north gate. As a result the openings of the patrol walk on the west half of the north wall are higher than those in the east half (3.60m compared with 3.10m). The twenty-seven openings in the north wall are in four groups of five or six between the corner towers, internal towers and the towers of the north gate.

In the east wall (191.25m between corner towers) there were seven openings at the upper level between the north-east tower and the internal tower, with the first narrower than the rest. Between the internal tower and the east gate, located offcentre 8m to the north, there are eight openings. What little remains of the west wall is enclosed on both sides by later buildings. Traces of doors through the thickness of the wall to the interval towers have been noted at ground and the upper level (at east tower of north wall), and of the doors through the angles of perimeter walls into the corner towers (at north-east tower). Between the north and south walls the height above ground of the cornice at the top of the perimeter wall increases from 17 to 24m.

On the south the forbidding aspect of a military fortress is replaced by the ornate and imposing façade of a great villa (Plate 6). At the upper level, 9m above the foundations (and 6m above modern ground level) the south façade fronts a covered gallery which ran the entire length of the south wall. Forty-two arcade openings are set between forty-four engaged columns of limestone blocks in the wall-courses. Each is surmounted by a half-capital which, save for the absence of a layer of acanthus leaves, matches closely the Corinthian capitals.[91]

The monotony of the gallery frontages is relieved by three *loggias*, one at the centre and one on either side adjoining the corner towers. Here the plain architrave was raised to an arch, above two larger columns spaced more widely than the rest. At two other places, roughly equidistant between the three *loggias*, the arched opening is slightly wider (2.55m), higher and embellished with a decorative moulding.[92] These enlarged openings are not placed symmetrically in the façade; that in the east is twelfth from the centre and tenth from the east; that in the west is placed *vice versa*. These locations were evidently determined by the axis of two principal chambers behind the gallery, on the west the large aisled chamber (no. 6, below p. ??52). whose pitched roof will have risen above the top of the south façade, and in the east that of the great Triclinium (17B; see below p. ??52). So that the gallery should have a height proportionate to its width (6.5m), the south wall is likely to have been raised above the *archivolts* of the *loggias* to give an interior height of 4.5m. A few traces of original masonry of the highest courses can still be detected in the masonry of later periods (see note 90).

Plate 6   South façade by Adam (1764).

Below the arcade the plain face of the wall was broken only by the narrow window slits, arched and splayed, which gave some light into the gallery basement.[93] In the centre at the lower level, the south gate was a simple entrance leading to the basements. The well-known reconstructions of the residence by Niemann and Hébrard depict the south wall at or close to the water's edge. Recent excavations near the south-east tower failed to show whether the sea did in fact lap up against the walls here.[94]

Three types of tower were bonded into the outer face of the perimeter walls, square corner towers, pairs of octagonal towers flanking the three landward gates and square interval towers in the intervals between these.

The four corner-towers were plain in appearance like the perimeter wall, with sides of approximately 12m and projecting 8.6m beyond the perimeter. Though their walls are not as thick (1.8m compared with 2.10m of the perimeter) the towers rose four metres higher. Three survive largely intact, that at the south-west corner being demolished *c.* 1550 after its foundations had been undermined by the sea. The two southern towers had four storeys, with two tapered and arched windows for each storey, except for the ground level which had window slits in the three open sides. The two in the north had only three storeys, an adjustment to the slope of the terrain. The towers were entered by narrow passages which turned a right-angle through the thickness of the perimeter wall, both at ground level and at the upper level of the patrol walk or, in the south, the long gallery. The north-west and south-east towers are best preserved. The former, once known as St Peter's Tower, was extensively damaged by fire in the last century but restored in 1914-15. Around half of the surviving north-east tower, now more fully exposed through clearance in recent years, is of original masonry. Recent excavations cleared the interior of the south-east tower, and exposed the passages leading through the perimeter wall at ground and at the upper level.[95]

In the north-west tower the floor level of the upper entrance passage was 0.7m below the bottom of the arched openings in the perimeter wall, indicating the level of the floor of the patrol walk. Access to the second floor was by a stairway 0.90m wide, with twenty-three steps within the south-west wall. It actually began within the thickness of the perimeter wall and was lit by a small semi-circular window. They may have continued to a third-floor level, indicated by four courses of masonry surviving above the cornice. The floors within the corner towers rested on timber joists and the roofs were of tile on timber beams.

Plate 7   North gate façade.

The six square interval towers have long since been removed, save for the northern tower on the west wall, now wholly enclosed by later buildings. A little of its enclosing wall is visible and it can be deduced that the internal north-south dimension was 5.85m, the wall 1.5m thick and its external north-south width *c*. 8.85m. Traces of the outer wall at basement level indicated a projection of *c*. 8.9m beyond the outer face of the perimeter. Each wall had an arched window at the same height as the corner towers. A 9m interruption of the cornice, which ran around all the towers, indicates the position of the northern interval tower on the east wall. In the seventeenth century the towers were preserved to a height above the Perimeter Wall, similar to that of the corner and gate towers.

Each of the three landward gates was flanked by octagonal towers engaged with the perimeter walls. The few traces of these which remain have survived through incorporation in later buildings but their dimensions and plan have been proved by recent excavations. Constructed in identical fashion to the corner and interval towers, they projected 10m beyond and rose 5m above the perimeter, with octagonal hipped roofs. Entrances led through the perimeter walls at ground and first-floor level, with access to the higher storeys by stairs in the thicknesses of the walls. Each of the eight sides was 3.56m long. At first-floor level the tower wall is 1.55m thick, decreasing in the upper levels. The third-floor level was around 1.80m above the capping cornice of the perimeter. Inside, the chambers of the gate towers were vaulted, shallower at the ground floor than the first. The upper floors had ceilings and floors of timber rafters similar to those in the towers.

GATES[95]

A single-passage gate was placed centrally in each of the four walls. The three landward gates were imposing entrances flanked by octagonal towers (described above). The south gate was a simple doorway from the basement level leading, one presumes, to a jetty alongside or close to the south wall. An ornate façade distinguishes the north gate (Plate 7) as the principal entrance — in a military sense the *porta praetoria* (see below p. 70) — which, like the other gates, has borne different names over the ages, none of which has an ancient origin. In medieval times the north gate was the 'Roman Gate' (*porta Romae*) but later was named 'Golden Gate' (*porta aurea*), first recorded in 1553. The east gate (militarily, the *porta principalis dextra*) was, around the same time, named 'Brazen Gate' (*Porta aenea*), but may have in antiquity been called 'Epetium Gate' from the small harbour settlement four miles away. Its medieval name was 'New Gate' (*porta nova*). The west gate, long known as the 'Iron Gate' (*porta ferrea*) was formerly called '*porta Franche*'. The medieval street between the east and west gates was long called 'Between the Double Gates' (*inter ambas portas*). The small south gate blocked for centuries is first recorded in 1553 with the name 'Silver Gate' (*porta argentea*). As late as 1846 the street then named Grota which led from it was still a cul-de-sac. It is a simple opening 3.7m high and *c.* 2m wide, with a horizontal lintel (now renewed) and surmounting arch similar to the landward gates.

The common feature of the three landward gates was an inner and outer entrance, separated by an open court around 9-10m square. The outer entrance had a portcullis which could be lowered in front of the inward-opening doors. At the upper level around the court the arched openings and a patrol walk were continued, save for the north side of the north gate. The upper floor was paved with stone slabs. On the inner sides of the gate, behind the octagonal towers, stairways led from the interior perimeter road to the patrol walk at the upper level.

At the north gate the two flanking towers are set 15m apart and the height from entrance threshold to the capping cornice is 14m. At the lower level a single arched entrance leads through the plain wall; the arch begins at 4.2m above the threshold and rises to 7.58m. Across the base of the arch there is a horizontal lintel of nine keyed *voussoirs*.[96] The projecting door-piers on either side narrow the entrance to 3.57m. The inner and outer faces of the arch have a running leaf decoration, egg-and-dart and bead-and-reel. On each side of the entrance a semi-circular niche was set in the wall, flanked by pilasters with Corinthian capitals. They rest on consols which spring from the wall more than is required. Their upper surfaces are plain and devoid of any markings that might indicate what had stood upon them. Half *cupolas* which crown the niches are formed of single blocks bonded with the wall surface, and are marked off from the rest of the niches by an egg-and-dart ornament.

At the upper level three pairs of consols once supported free-standing columns, on which rested a blind arcade. Above this runs the capping cornice of the perimeter wall. The undersides of the flanking pairs of consols are decorated with acanthus leaves, and of the central pair with animal heads with long ears and curly hair.[97] Attic bases are worked on the consols to which the columns were attached with dowels. Directly below the consols runs a small moulded cornice, interrupted by the heads of the two lower niches and the arch of the entrance. The outer sides of the end consols hidden behind the octagonal towers, were left unworked. A heavy cornice, with leaf *torus* decoration, ran up to the end consol on either side. Evidently these were the ends of a heavy cornice which encircled the towers, not present on the corner or interval towers, and embraced them in the decorative scheme of the gate. Above the missing columns at the upper level, between their capitals and base of the arches, runs a projecting order, with the moulding of an architrave and bonded into the face of the wall. It is continued along the intervening face of the wall and the interior of the three niches. The centre niche is shallow and rectangular, those at the sides semicircular with *cupolas* of single blocks bonded with the wall courses. The seven arches, of which the two between the niches are slightly larger than the rest, project 0.5m from the wall and have plain stepped mouldings.

Finally atop the cornice are four plinths (a fifth may have disappeared) whose varying heights (from left to right: 0.62m, 0.75m, 0.82m and 0.61m) are suggestive of a hierarchy, possibly of the Tetrarchy.[98] The niches, arcades and bases of the north gate form a scheme that must have conveyed a message through images set in an architectural frame. The loss of the statues and, possibly, inscriptions, denies us any real comprehension of what was once perhaps the most expressive image of the entire residence (Figure 3). Behind the façade, plain walls similar to the perimeter, 2.6-3.3m thick with rubble core, surround the court which is 9m square. The walkway across the north side of the gate has been occupied by a chapel since medieval times, its outer wall being pierced only by two window slits between the niches.

At the rear of the court the inner entrance was similar to the outer, though the horizontal lintel is no longer in place. At the upper level the waist cornice continues above the arch of the entrance and above these are visible three arched openings (now blocked up) of the walkway. In the west wall of the court are traces of the stairs, resting on a brick vault and lit by a window-slit, leading from the court to the upper level of the gates.

The west gate, best preserved of the landward gates, is largely concealed by later buildings (Plate 8). Though, like the east gate, of similar plan and structure to the north gate, it lacks some of the latter's decoration and ornate façade. The arch of the entrance has a plain moulding. A winged victory carved on the central *voussoir* was replaced in medieval times by a St John's Cross. The two niches at the lower level either side of the entrance are now concealed. At the upper level the gate was a continuation of the upper walkway with five arched openings. The court, 10.6m wide and 9.3m deep, the entrances 3.6m wide, is more or less intact and traces of the flanking octagonal towers have been detected within the fabric of later buildings. The outer entrance is virtually intact, along with traces of its means of closure, a lowered grill and double doors. On the piers of the entrance a slot 0.2m wide and 0.16m deep corresponds exactly with the slot through the horizontal lintel and the surmounting arch. The outer *voussoirs* of the former were notched, the inner ones had straight joints. The doors were fitted to a recess of 0.3m behind the piers in which the slot for the grill is cut. An upper pivot socket is preserved in a projecting stone of the north pier. The entrance (whose threshold is 2.4m lower than that of the north gate) was originally 5.14m high.

Figure 3   Reconstruction of north gate (*porta aurea*).

A simple moulded cornice ran above the arches around the four sides of the court, corresponding to the floor level of the upper walkway, and formed of its floor-slabs projecting through the wall. In the floor a round hole 0.3m in diameter was connected with the lowering and raising of the grill. Remains of stairs suggested an arrangement for access from ground to upper level similar to those at the north gate.

What is now to be seen of the east gate is the result of restoration following bomb damage.[99] It had already been largely demolished when a church (now destroyed) was erected on the site, which incorporated part of its outer wall. The foundations of the court and piers of the inner entrance have been located. The width of the entrance was 3.5m and, at 2.9m, the wall thicknesses are less than at the other gates. At the upper level are the five openings of the walkway. The axis of the central opening does not coincide with that of the entrance below, an asymmetry found also at the west gate. This curiosity, uncharacteristic of earlier Roman architecture, is not easily

Plate 8   West gate by Cassas (1782).

explained. It is more likely to be a simple neglect of symmetry through haste in construction than a deliberately contrived image of restlessness.

PERIMETER BUILDINGS[100]

Along the inside of the north wall and the northern halves of the east and west walls were ranges of two-storey buildings facing onto a narrow perimeter street. The upper storey looked onto the walkway through windows in the outer wall. The lower level was built against the solid face of the Perimeter Wall and looked out through arcades on the perimeter street. The inner façade of the perimeter buildings rested upon stone piers, set *c.* 2.6m apart and 10-11m from the inner face of the perimeter wall. Behind these piers partition walls *c.* 3.50m apart abutted the perimeter wall and extended for around half the distance between the wall and the piers, until they were closed off by a front wall. The small chambers were evidently magazines and each was entered by a door from the covered passage behind the piers. Five magazines have been recognised against the west wall, just south of the north-west angle, and recently excavation has proved the existence of similar magazines behind the three surviving piers roughly half-way between the east gate and the north-east tower.[101] If their dimensions were roughly the same then there would have been around sixty magazines around the northern perimeter between the east and west gates.

Arrangements at the upper level still remain largely unknown. Presumably the upper floor followed the same level as the walkway in the perimeter wall. This follows the level of the upper cornice, falling from its highest point at the north-east corner. Most likely rafters were laid from one partition to the other and covered with floorboards. The cornice is much too close to the top of the arched openings in the perimeter wall to allow any vault or elaborate roof construction. Most likely roof trusses were rested on the cornice for a flat or pent roof of tiles. There is no evidence for any interconnection between magazines at the ground level and the upper level of the perimeter, save by the stairs flanking the main gates. This suggests that the two levels had functions which were largely unrelated — at ground level stores and equipment, at the upper level some facilities for guards patrolling the roughly one hundred-metre sections of the perimeter.

The arcades around the perimeter faced on to a street which ran around the northern half of the interior — approximating to the intervallum road (*via sagularis*) of Roman forts. If this took up the full width of the intervening space between the arcades and the interior buildings of the northern interior then it will have been around 10m wide. At the intersections of the perimeter road with the colonnades of the principal streets, at the north gate and on north sides of the east and west gate, there was a four-way arch (tetrapylon), the piers of which are known west of the north gate and north of the west gate.

Earlier reconstructions made the not unreasonable assumption that the perimeter street had continued south of the east-west street as far as the north wall of the private apartments. That has now been ruled out, certainly on the east and probably on the west, by the courtyard which fills the area between the east wall of the mausoleum temenos and the three piers around 10m from the inner face of the east perimeter wall.[102] Similarly the position of the west baths behind the temple temenos appears to rule out any southward continuation of the perimeter street on the west also (see below p. 57).

STREETS AND BUILDINGS IN NORTHERN INTERIOR (Figure 4)

The two northern quarters of the interior were demarcated by two paved streets, one between the east and west gates, the other from the north gate to a junction with the cross-street at the centres.[103] As has often been observed, they correspond to a familiar arrangement of streets in legionary fortresse, and auxiliary forts, the *via praetoria* from the north gate (*porta praetoria*) and the *via principalis* between the west gate (*porta principalis sinistra*) and the east gate (*porta principalis dextra*). At the centre, opposite the junction of these streets, would be placed the headquarters (*principia*) including the military, shrine (*aedes principiorum*). In Diocletian's residence the corresponding place was taken up by the peristyle and, specifically that of the shrine, by the monumental porch to the private apartments (see below p 43) [104]

Both streets were more than 10m wide and flanked with covered colonnades, their Corinthian columns and capitals supporting a horizontal architrave with plain stepped moulding. The beginning of the colonnade is preserved on the north pier of the west gate, and other remains, including a Corinthian column and fragment of architrave of the east-west street came to light after destruction by fire in 1924 of buildings adjoining the mausoleum precinct.[105] At the central intersection remains of three of the four corner piers have been located, with that at the north-east corner now restored within the 'Diocletian Café' which was erected over the site. Excavations in

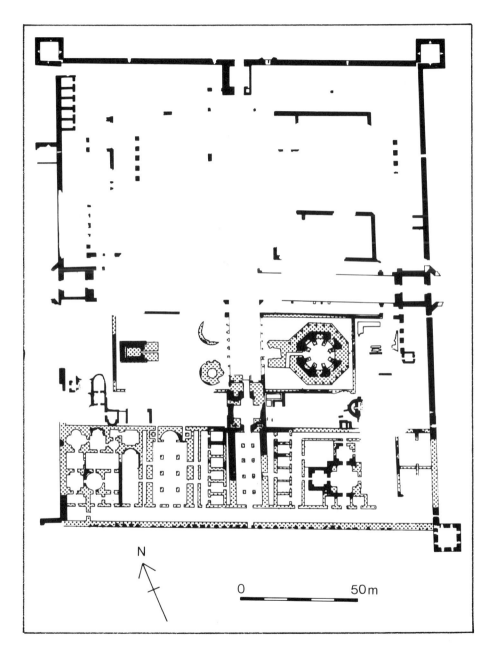

Figure 4   Recorded remains of Diocletian's Palace (1972), based on *Split Excavation* 1,
drawing 14. Structures at ground level indicated in black, at basement level in
grey.

39

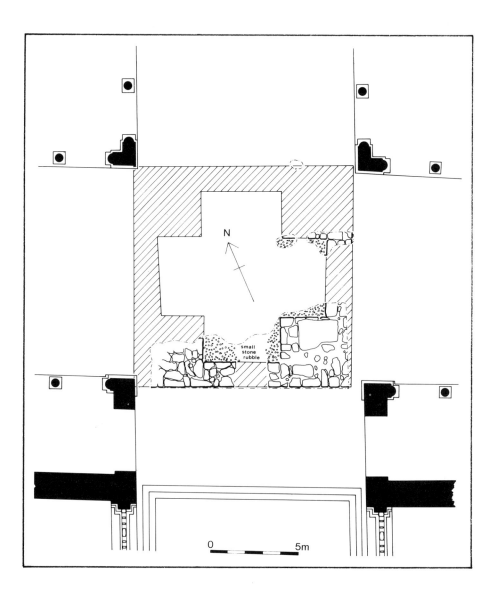

Figure 5 *Decussis* at central street intersection Composite plan based on B. Gabričević,
VAHD 63-4 (1961-62), 1969, 113 ff.

1960 at the intersection revealed at a depth of 0.8m below the ancient paving a cruciform design marked out by a border of large stones (Figure 5). The arms are *c*. 9.5m long and *c*. 4.25m wide. It has been identified as a *decussis*, a fixed point of intersection used by surveyors, by which the positions and width of the gates and the alignment of the colonnaded streets were determined.[106] Architectural consistency suggests that the architrave was raised to an arch opposite the principal entrances to the building behind the colonnades in the north-west and north-east quarters.

The buildings in the northern half of the interior are the least known, though what is known of both blocks appears sufficient to rule out the existence of any minor street, such as an east-west street midway between the main cross-street and the north wall.[107] Both blocks in the northern interior occupied rectangles 60 by 45m. That in the north-west was built around a rectangular court, of which remains of five piers from the west side have been identified. Traces of the footings of the west, north and east external walls have been located, also remains of a covered drain around the west, north and east sides, between the outer wall and the piers of the court. The east building was centred on a court but truncated on the north and south by ranges of rooms 15m wide. The mosaic located in front of the Church on the south side of Gregory of Nin Square (*Grga Ninski poljana*), with a simple geometric pattern, lay in the middle room of the south range.[108] The solid masonry has suggested that these buildings may have risen to the level of the perimeter walls with upper storeys possibly better appointed than those at ground level. If piers on the west wall of the north-west block indicate a link between it and the walkway at the upper level of the perimeter, it is possible that it functioned as barracks; while the mosaic in the east has led to a suggestion that it served, at least in part, 'a ceremonial purpose'.[109] Conceivably the record that that part was later adapted as a state textile factory (*gynaecium*) may indicate that such an activity was already carried on when it was still Diocletian's private residence (see below p. 83).

PERISTYLE[110]

The line of the colonnaded street from the north gate is continued south of its junction with the east-west cross street by a paved court flanked by arcades, 27m long and 13.50m wide (Plate 9). Long known as Cathedral Square, it has since 1920 been generally known as peristyle (*peristil*), from its flanking columns 5.25m high (Plate 10). Twelve of the columns are of red Egyptian granite, the remainder of marble which may be Euboean cipollino. These have long had to be strengthened by bronze hoops, after having split beneath the weight of the arcades and massive and ornate architrave. Though the peristyle is treated now as an architectural unity at the centre of the residence, this is perhaps mainly due to its remarkable survival as an open space.[111] In fact it is formed by the monumental façades of the three principal elements which occupy the southern half of the interior — on the south the monumental porch leading to the private apartments (Plate 11), on the east the entrance to the mausoleum precinct and on the west that to the temple precinct.

The intervals between the columns of the lateral arcades were closed by a balustrade, stone panels carved to a lattice pattern (*transennae*), to a height of 2.40m. At least one panel apparently remained *in situ* when the drawing in Adam's volume was made. All that now remains is a projection on the column base to which it was secured, and another between the two columns on the lowest of the steps rising to the Cathedral. The entrances to the mausoleum and temple precincts were marked by a slightly wider spacing of the columns. The three southernmost arches on either side (which begin with the precinct entrances) are slightly higher than the rest, almost touching the surmounting architrave.

Plate 9   Model of peristyle and mausoleum (Niemann)

Plate 10   South arcade of peristyle.

The south side of the peristyle is formed by the huge entrance porch to the private apartments. A great pediment rests on four columns of red granite surmounted by Corinthian capitals. Above the wider interval between the inner pair of columns the horizontal architrave is raised to an arch, serving to focus attention on the centre of the porch, where the doorway at the back of the porch led to the great vestibule. Since it was first recorded by Adam the familiar view had included also a pair of renaissance chapels set between columns either side of the central opening.[117] Above the apex of the pediment there is a stone plinth 4.26m wide which will presumably have supported a group of statuary, perhaps a four-horse chariot (*quadriga*).

Recent excavations (1959–60) have significantly increased our knowledge of the original appearance and function of the peristyle.[118] Around the north, east and west sides three steps led down to the paved floor (Figure 6). In its original state the peristyle presented the image of the classical temple turned inside-out. Most significant, it was discovered that on the south two banks of steps led up to the porch, probably corresponding in width to the two lateral openings between the four columns of the porch. The central opening was

Diocletian's Palace, Split: Residence of a Retired Roman Emperor

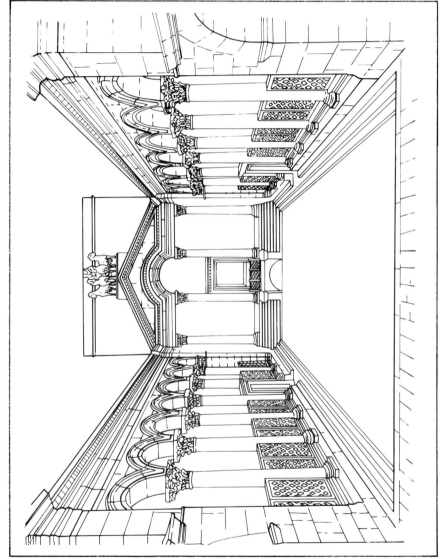

Figure 6   Reconstruction of the Peristyle.

44

Plate 11 Entrance porch to private apartments.

fronted by a low balustrade of stone panels carved in a lattice pattern (*transennae*) to make the form of a tribunal. Below this, instead of the rising steps, was a vaulted opening beneath which steps led down from the peristyle to the basement level beneath the Vestibule and then to the south gate, in the lower level of the perimeter wall.[114]

Excavations beneath the paving of the peristyle revealed something of the extensive systems of drainage. A principal culvert led from north to south down the centre, collecting on the way smaller channels from the mausoleum and temple enclosures, then beneath the basements to an outflow in the sea.

MAUSOLEUM[115]

The east side of the peristyle was the arcaded frontage of the rectangular precinct 32–33m wide and 39m deep. The remaining three walls were of plain masonry (and the southernmost 6.5m of the west wall) and rose to the same height as the peristyle architrave. Their inner face contained in their thicknesses alternating round and square niches which, one may suppose, once held statues. The enclosure was a sacred precinct (*temenos*) designed to enclose the great octagonal Mausoleum of Diocletian. In ancient times it will have only been visible through the grills of the peristyle balustrade and the only entrance was the doorway from the peristyle between the fifth and sixth columns (from the north).

By an irony of history, the last resting place of the Great Persecutor is now the Cathedral of Split, a conversion brought about by Archbishop John of Ravenna in the early Middle Ages (see below p. 86). This will have doubtless been the occasion for the removal, wherever possible, of any surviving remains that will have recalled the devout pagan. Today the mausoleum appears the best-preserved part of the residence, though this is partly due to a comprehensive restoration in the late nineteenth century, (1880–85), when the capitals and some of the columns from the interior were replaced and the originals removed to the Archaeological Museum.

The mausoleum is an octagon with sides each of 7.60m and walls 2.75m thick built of close-fitting blocks (Plate 12). It rested upon a larger octagonal podium 3.70m high; within the podium there is a domed crypt *c.* 13m in diameter, whose interior is reduced by eight projecting buttresses. On the west of the podium there was an extension of *c.* 9m on which the entrance porch was erected. A narrow passage *c.* 1m wide entered the side of the podium of the porch near its south-west corner. It led northwards as far as a right-angled corner, after which one entered the crypt from the west on the main east-west axis of the mausoleum. A recent study of the crypt, which was lit — or rather ventilated — by three tapering slits to the top of the podium just outside the Mausoleum superstructure, appears to suggest that the chamber can have served no formal purpose and was certainly not the repository, for

Plate 12   Mausoleum from northeast after fire in 1924. *Photo: Bulić-Karaman*, pl.26a.

Diocletian's sarcophagus.[116] Its interior was undecorated and the floor consisted of rough stone blocks, which formed part of the raft on which the podium of the mausoleum and porch was erected. The passage was never closed by a door and may have been permanently sealed after construction, in which case the window slits were intended merely to ventilate the sealed chamber. If, on the other hand, a well in the floor is of Roman date, either Diocletianic or later, then there must have been some permanent means of access to it.

The site of the mausoleum sloped southwards. To counter this a raft of two layers of roughly squared blocks on a layer of stone rubble was retained on the south by the foundation of the temenos wall. The interior of the temenos may have been paved or possibly laid out as a garden. The entrance to the Mausoleum in the west side had a richly decorated doorframe, a vine-scroll inhabited with heads of animals. The jambs rise to terminate in massive consols on which rests the richly carved horizontal lintel. Virtually all remains of the entrance porch were obliterated by construction of the renaissance belfry (thirteenth to seventeenth centuries), which was rebuilt at the end of the last century,. There are some traces of the bank of sixteen steps 2.80m wide, which led from the doorway to the peristyle up to the level of the podium.

In the footings of the belfry, traces remain of the eight supporting columns of the porch, four in the façade with the others set behind. The roof and façade of the porch may have presented a smaller version of the great porch fronting the vestibule. This matter is complicated by the existence of a semi-circular window, formed by the arch above the doorway, which will have been obscured if the pediment was raised to contain an arch above the central opening between the columns. Since the window appears to have been the only source of light to the interior, it could hardly have been blocked by the porch roof. Moreover, the problem of the porch roof and façade is further complicated by the need of match up with the pent roof and architrave of the surrounding ambulatory (*peripteron*).[117]

The circular chamber of the mausoleum has a diameter of 13.35m and rises to 21.5m at the centre of its dome (Plate 13). At ground level there are four semi-circular and four square niches set alternately in the wall, one of the latter housing the opening for the entrance on the west side.[118] Between each pair of niches eight columns of red Egyptian granite (Assuan) were set 0.56m from the wall. Each was surmounted by a Corinthian capital and topped with a projecting order reaching a height of 9.06m. Directly upon this, and without bases, stood eight smaller columns and capitals (four composite, four neo-

Plate 13   Mausoleum interior from west. *Photo: Bulić-Karaman*, pl.43.

Corinthian) surmounted by another projecting architrave reaching a height of 4.85m. Four of these (at the cardinal points) are of imperial porphyry, the other four of grey Egyptian granite and another stone. The two orders together reach the beginning of the dome at 13.91m. The columns have no structural function and were inserted in the completed shell of the mausoleum. The arrangements of columns within the chamber correspond to eight of the twenty-four which originally formed the portico at the edge of the podium.[119]

The hemispherical dome rises 1.25m above the upper cornice and remains intact. It was constructed of bricks of inferior quality made by a local factory bearing the stamp DALMATI. These are set in small arcs to give a feather-pattern, one rising above the other, until the dome is completed by bricks set in decreasing circles. The outer cover was an eight-sided tiled roof, capped by a pine-cone resting on four beasts.[120]

The attractive patterns of bricks in the dome were probably once covered by mosaic decoration which may have extended to the walls and niches (see above p. 19). Restoration in the last century, established that the dome was always closed and never had an opening (*oculus*) at the centre (a feature by this time obsolete in Roman architecture). Within the thickness of the dome a passage for maintenance rises by twenty-four steps from near the second upper column to the right of the entrance. The chamber had a floor of black and white marble, 0.18m below the present surface. Nothing remains of any original arrangements for the burial of Diocletian or members of his family. The historian Ammianus Marcellinus records, among a catalogue of intrigue and accusations at the court of Constantius II, the report of a theft and concealment in AD 356 of the purple robe (*velamen purpureum*) from Diocletian's tomb. It has been suggested that some fragments of porphyry now in the Archaeological Museum once belonged to the sarcophagus of Diocletian.[121]

Around the Mausoleum a covered portico rested on twenty-four columns, re-used and in a variety of marbles and granites, surmounted by Corinthian capitals.[122] A tiled pent roof rested upon an architrave with plain stepped moulding and beamsockets in the outer face of the mausoleum. The inner ceiling was of stone slabs covered with mouldings enclosing masks and rosettes. Four of these remain *in situ*, three on the north and one on the south, and several others have been discovered among debris during restoration work.

Apart from the carved ornament of column capitals and cornices, the sole authentic decoration surviving in the mausoleum is a carved stone frieze behind the capitals of the upper order.[123] Much of it consists of hunting scenes with Erotes, garlands and masks. Three crudely executed human faces are set within wreaths held by Erotes, reminiscent of decoration on Roman sarcophagi. Above the square niche opposite the entrance, at the end of the fourth and at the beginning of the sixth panel, are busts of a woman with elaborate coiffeur and a man clad in what appears a toga and with a crown or wreath on his head (Plate 14). They have long been identified with

Plate 14   Head of Diocletian (?) in Mausoleum frieze. *Photo: Town Planning Institute, Split.*

Diocletian and his wife Prisca (she never received the dignity of Augusta or empress), a victim of Licinius in AD 315 (see above p. 11). The third portrait is the winged head of Hermes the Conductor of Souls (*Psychopompus*), who guided the spirits of the dead on their journey to the underworld of Hades. The mausoleum is often compared with several other buildings of the same era — notably the great rotunda at Thessalonica, which was probably intended as the Mausoleum of Galerius, though in the event it was not used for this purpose. A closer parallel is furnished by the Mausoleum of Maxentius on the Via Appia near Rome. It stands on a podium within a temenos and has alternating semi-circular and rectangular niches.[124] Though like the rotunda at Thessalonica converted to a Christian church, Diocletian's Mausoleum remains among the best authentic surviving monuments of Late Roman architecture.

TEMPLE

The precinct west of the peristyle was 44m deep (5m more than that of the mausoleum) and is now known to have contained not only the well-known small classical temple but two smaller circular structures, also perhaps shrines, in the north-east and southeast angles. The temple faces east towards the mausoleum across the peristyle, though the alignment is not precise. Steps flanked by piers ascend a podium 21 by 9.30m wide and 2.5m high, but nothing now remains of the six columns of the temple porch (*pronaos*). The arrangement was tetrastyle in prostyle, with four columns in the front on which rested a triangular pediment fronting the ridged roof (Figure 7).

Possibly the pediment was undecorated, perhaps with no more than the formal architectural ornament one finds on the surviving pediment at the rear and on the great porch in the peristyle. Save for the porch and its tiled roof, the temple is intact, perhaps the best-preserved example of the small classical temple in the Roman style.[126]

The outer walls of the chamber (*cella*, 11.40m long) are of plain, close-fitting blocks, with pilasters and capitals at the corners (Plate 15). After demolition of attached houses in 1907 the rear façade was found to be intact. The plain gable has a wreath at the centre. Between the surviving square pilasters (*antae*) and capitals, which project for *c.* 1.50m, the doorway, 6m high and 2.5m wide, has a richly carved frame. Amid leafy tendrils children pick bunches of grapes as birds fly around. Above the lintel a Corinthian cornice rests on two voluted consols. On its underside, divided by ten brackets (modillions), are heads of two Tritons (half-fish and half-human marine deities), Helios (the sun), Hercules and Apollo, also an eagle, another human face and two winged victories. Nothing in the surviving ornament of the temple can be related specifically to Diocletian and his regime, unless it be a taste for the traditional images of Roman paganism. Inside the chamber (7.27 by 5.86m) the eye is now drawn immediately to the barrel vault above (Plate 16). This is made of three rows of closefitting carved slabs 0.60m thick, rough and unfinished on the outside but on the inside carved to give a ceiling with sixty-four coffers, eight rows in each direction.

The carved borders and central figures — human heads or rosettes — have often been compared with those of the Temple of Venus and Rome, built under Hadrian near the Forum on what had been the atrium of Nero's Golden

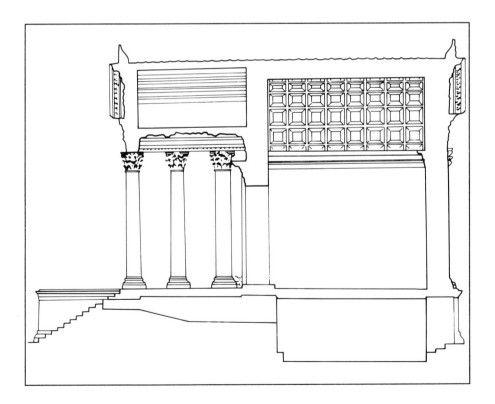

Figure 7   Cross-section of Temple, based on Marasović *Diocletian Palace*, Supplement
fig. 33.

Plate 15   Temple by Adam (1764).

House. Between the vault and the plain walls a Corinthian cornice runs around the three walls away from the entrance, the undersides of its modillions decorated with sheaves of thunderbolts. Like the mausoleum, the temple podium enclosed a crypt, entered by a narrow passage through the rear. Its function, if it ever had one, remains unknown. The temple was placed well to the rear of its precinct and its rear wall lay less than 2m from the inner face of the precinct wall.

It is recorded that a statue was removed from the temple and transported to Venice at the end of the fourteenth century. If it was the cult statue which the temple will have certainly housed, then one can assume that it was an image of Diocletian's Jupiter. That is suggested also by the carved figures on the underside of the cornice above the lintel, Jupiter's eagle and his heroic servant Hercules. The former is also indicated by his thunderbolts on the interior cornice. The knot of Hercules also figures in the carved architrave, as it does evidently on capitals at Piazza Armerina.

Plate 16 Barrel vault roof of temple from east. *Photo: Town Planning Institute, Split.*

Post-war excavations have revealed the existence of two circular structures in the eastern angles of the temple temenos, which have been identified as the remaining two shrines referred to in a sixteenth-century, account referring to four temples 'within the palace'. In the south-east angle restoration of medieval buildings revealed the moulded plinth of a circular structure, with a diameter of 9.25m and containing a small crypt. Fragments of its coffered ceiling and sculptured frieze were also discovered. The northern of the pair lies beneath the 'Café Luxor' but it was possible to establish that it was similar in plan and dimensions to the other. There seems no doubt that these circular buildings were part of the original design and they may have fulfilled some subordinate role to the classical temple. They could have been shrines but possibly roofed circles of columns (*monopteroi*) intended to house free-standing statues.[127]

VESTIBULE[128]

Beyond the great entrance porch on the south of the Peristyle lay a magnificent circular chamber, 12m across and 17m high to the centre of the dome, long known as the vestibule. The present opening in the dome is not an original oculus and the chamber was lit only by small arched windows (now blocked up) high in the walls. The walls were constructed not of dressed ashlar but of rough pieces of limestone set in mortar with alternating courses of brick (*opus incertum mixtum*). At ground level there were four round niches set diagonally to the north-south axis. Both the doorway leading from the porch and that on the south leading into the great entrance chamber (*tablinum*) had ornate frames set within arched openings. Even in its present mutilated state, the vestibule has a grandeur which matches the great porch on its north. The dome, and perhaps most of the walls, were once covered with mosaic of coloured glass, the rest with veneers of white and coloured marbles.[179]

The rotunda of the vestibule is enclosed within a square construction. This allowed space for spiral stairways to upper and lower levels. In the south-east one rose up to the full height of the dome, another down to the chamber below, the basement chamber to which the steps led down from the peristyle below the centre of the entrance porch.[130]

BATHS

Recent excavations have revealed that the narrow intervals between the two precincts and the private apartments on the south and perimeter wall to the east and west were occupied by two suites of baths, along with associated courts (*palaestrae*) and service areas.

The west baths, first located in 1959, were recently examined and the remains surveyed under conditions of considerable difficulty (Figure 8). Only the lower floors of the hypocausts, pilae of bricks and walls (*c.* 0.9m thick) mostly of brick up to and slightly above the level of the upper floors survive. Five rooms were identified, three on a north-south axis and each based on a square of *c.* 4.90m, though differing in plan. Another room adjoined on the north-west and the fifth on the south-east. All the rooms, except that on the south-east which was inaccessible, were found to have hypocaust heating. In

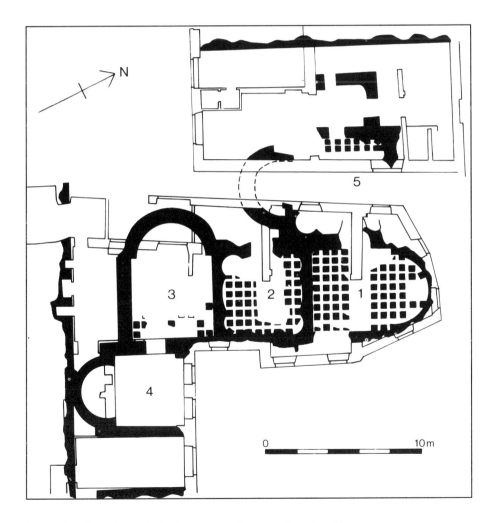

Figure 8   Plan of west baths, based on *Split Excavations* 2, p.55.

the most northerly room there was the arched opening through the apse leading from a furnace (*praefurnium*) on the north side of the baths. Nothing of the superstructure could be inferred from the debris removed during clearance, except for marble revetment and mosaics indicated by many fragments and coloured tesserae.[131]

Much less is known of the east baths. Excavation beneath a small square (Kraj Sv. Duje) outside the south-east of the Mausoleum precinct revealed the apse and part of an adjoining square room.[132] Both apse and room had hypocaust heating, that of the former surviving more or less intact. This upper floor rested upon carved stone pillars, and the hot gases entered from the furnace by an arch at the centre of the apse. It appears to have served as a marble-lined hot-water basin for the large heated chamber adjoining on the east. On the outside of the apse around the furnace was the fuel yard. Beneath this was found a section of lead pipe 60mm in diameter which conveyed water to the tank (situated above the furnace) which fed the basin.

There seems little doubt that both sets of baths were part of the original Diocletianic scheme, though positive evidence was only forthcoming from excavation of the east baths. Here the foundations were found to rest directly upon the levelled bedrock and a coin of Maximianus (286–305) was found at the floor-level of the fuel yard. Perhaps conclusive are the four curved entablature blocks from the apse (re-used in later buildings), whose mouldings resemble closely those of the mausoleum.[133]

It appears that most of the narrow spaces around the precincts were occupied by the baths and associated buildings. Certainly the discoveries have ruled out any continuation of the perimeter road south of the east-west street. A rectangular area (19.00 by 14.25m) east of the mausoleum precinct was bounded on the east by the piers of the arcade belonging to the inner façade of the perimeter buildings. Here covered porticos fronted by columns around the open court were floored with mosaic pavements of geometric design and it appears most likely that the area was an exercise yard (*palaestra*) — perhaps one of several — connected with the east baths.[134] At the other end of the area occupied by the baths, three similar though smaller mosaic floors were located around a small court just east of the vestibule basement, between the mausoleum temenos and the private apartments.[135] They lay at an intermediate level between the upper floors and basement level and perhaps were part of the baths, though it must have been a singularly gloomy and cheerless court, surrounded on three sides by sheer walls rising more than 20 metres.

PRIVATE APARTMENTS[136]

The area reserved for the actual residence of the retired Augustus was a block *c.* 40m wide, which extended from east to west perimeter wall behind the south façade. This whole complex rested upon vaulted basements up to 8m high. Most of these, and the upper floor they supported, remain intact.

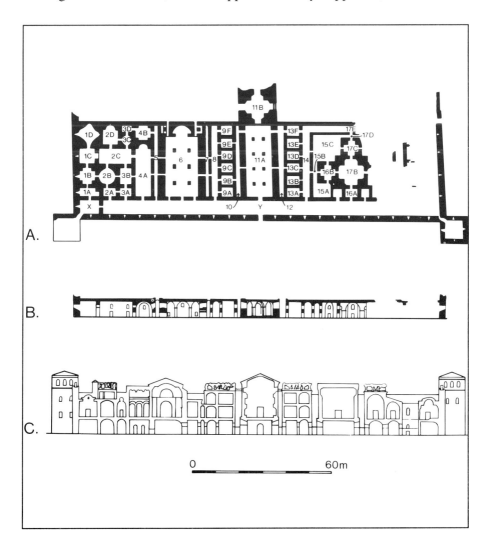

Figure 9   Plan (A), cross-section (B) and restored cross-section (C) of imperial apartments and basements.

There are few surviving remains of the apartments at the upper level but what does survive suffices to indicate that the upper chambers were similar in size, shape and arrangement to those of the basements (Figure 9). Clearance of the basements is now virtually complete, save at the east end where the general collapse of the vaults makes excavation a difficult undertaking.[137]

Plate 17   Central basement hall looking towards south gate. *Photo: Town Planning Institute, Split.*

The only formal entrance to the private apartments — that is save for small service stairs and passages — was that from the south of the circular vestibule. This led to a long chamber (11 A) 31m long and 12m wide, which was in effect a continuation of the peristyle (Plate 17). One cannot presume that the rows of piers at basement level were repeated at the upper level. The thick walls suggest that the chamber may have been spanned by a barrel vault, continuing the idiom of the peristyle. The inner faces of the walls were set with niches and the interior was lit by windows high in the walls. The chamber linked the vestibule on the north to the long gallery of the south façade, which gave the only access to the private apartments. The ornate outer frame of the south doorway to the gallery survives intact in the fabric of a standing building.[138]

The vestibule basement (11 B) has openings in all four sides, those on the east and west leading towards the east and west baths. The basement of the entrance hall (11 A) has walls and piers of limestone blocks supporting tufa vaults. The chamber is lit by four tapering windows at a height of 2m from the light-wells on either side (10 and 12). Above the wall-blocks the first 1.25m of the vaults are of brick, and courses of bricks are continued across the vaults between the rows of tufa *voussoirs*. The arches for niches, doorways and windows are of two rows of bricks set on end. The vaulted basement of the gallery (Y) was lit by window slits through the perimeter wall. At both basement and residential level access to all chambers was by the gallery.

Beyond the light-wells (10 and 12) flanking the entrance hall (11 A) are rows of small chambers *c*. 5.25 by 4.30m, six on the west (9 A-F) and six on the east (13A-F). Each is roofed with a barrel vault and was entered from a vaulted corridor (8 and 14) on the sides away from the light-wells.[140] On the east a complex of rooms, corridors and light-wells (14, 15, 16 and 17) has been recognised from the basement remains as the principal dining-room (*triclinium*). At the upper level enough survives to show that the great central chamber (17 B) was an octagonal hall (square on the outside) recessed with niches.[141] The north-south axis coincides with the wider opening and vaulted architrave at the eleventh opening from the centre in the south façade. The block was enclosed on three sides by a vaulted corridor, on the west (14) and on the north (17 E). Onto the former open the six small chambers (13 A-F) flanking the entrance hall. On the south three small antechambers (16 A, 17 A and 18 A) link the main chamber with the long gallery. Within the angles formed by the surrounding corridor large areas around the triclinium remained open to the sky down to the basement floor level.[142]

On the west of the entrance hall, the small chambers (9 A-F) and corridor (8) lay the largest chamber in the private apartments, measuring 32 by 14m (6). Known for many years as Pavissić, its intersecting vaults rest on six massive piers, forming three aisles with a central apse to the north. It was flanked by narrow light-wells (S and 7) down to basement level and had three entrances from the gallery.[143] It may have been the principal reception room of the apartments and, whatever its function, is likely to have played an important role in their working (see further p. 73). At the west end of the range a square of roughly 30m by 30m was occupied by fourteen small chambers. Recent clearance of debris from the basements has revealed the variety of their plans, rectangular with and without apses, circular, cruciform and simple square. In the south-east of this block was a rectangular hall (4 A) with an apse on the north (of which some remains survive at the upper level), and a single entrance from the gallery. North of this but unconnected with it, a small chamber of cruciform shape (4 B) was entered by a doorway from the light-well (5). This led to a tiny rectangular room on the west (3 D) and a small circular chamber (3 C) south of that. West of the rectangular hall with apse (4 A) lay a circular chamber (2 B) surrounded by seven square or rectangular chambers of varrying size (1 A–C, 2 A and C, and 3 A–B). In the largest of these, a rectangular chamber (2 C), it was evident that timber was employed, either during construction or even to counter subsequent weakness.[144]

West of this room was an arched entrance wider than the normal basement doorway leading to a smaller square chamber (1 C), not yet wholly cleared of debris. All five basement chambers adjoining the west perimeter wall (Room X at the end of the gallery Y, and 1 A–D) were lit by window-slits through the wall located centrally in each chamber. North of the rectangular room (2 C) a small square room with an apse on the north side survived partly at the upper level, where the apse was revealed to contain three semi-circular niches not present at basement level. The circular room (2 B) had at the upper level alternating rectangular and circular niches. With the triclinium identified in the east range, this block of chambers at the west end may with reasonable certainty be identified as the private dwelling rooms of Diocletian.

AQUEDUCT[145]

In a land notorious for shortage of water, wells and cisterns were no doubt used within the residence, but an adequate and uninterrupted supply could only be guaranteed by an aqueduct from the river Jadro, which had for centuries been the principal source of water for the city of Salona.[146] Typical of rivers in the limestone karst of Dalmatia, honeycombed with caves and underground channels, the Jadro emerges in full spate from a spur of the Mosor mountain south of Klis at a height of 36m above sea level. From here it was conveyed for *c.* 9.7km to the North Gate of the residence. At a few places in this course it rests on arches in the well-known Roman fashion, of which the best known section on twenty-eight arches reaching a height of 16.5m crosses a dry valley — the 'dry-bridge' (Suhi Most) in Dujmovaca (Plate 18). For most of its course it lies below ground, in one place (Ravne Njive) cut into the rock up to 21m deep. The normal flow is 13 cubic metres per second, that is 1.1 million cubic metres each twenty-four hours.[147]

Plate 18 Aqueduct before restoration in 1878.

Nothing is known of its distribution. Most likely a reservoir existed near the north gate, whence channels or pipes conveyed it to different parts. The overflow presumably ran down the main drain beneath the peristyle and basements.[148] One can only speculate if the provision of such a large amount of water had been stipulated by Diocletian as in part a necessary amenity for his vegetable garden, of which he is reputed to have boasted after four years of retirement.[149]

CHAPTER 4

THE IMPERIAL VILLA

'PALATIAL' AND 'CEREMONIAL' INTERPRETATIONS

By formally divesting himself of his imperial robe at the ceremony of abdication, Diocletian became once more a private citizen. The years of his retirement were passed in his villa, and that term is applied consistently to the residence at Split in the late Roman accounts of his death.[150] All that is recorded of his last years affords no support for any assumption that Split ever served as a *Palatium,* the great complexes devised for the court ceremonial and household of a reigning emperor. Since the remains of Split were described by Niemann and by Hébrard and Zeiller early this century some scholars have looked on Split as a precursor of the traditions of palatial architecture of the Late Roman and Byzantine Empire. These notions have been based on the significance attached to such features as the intersecting colonnaded streets, the peristyle, the monumental porch, vestibule and the aisled chamber that lay behind it. It would obviously be unwise to ignore the elements of Split which do appear to resemble the rotundas and basilicas, vestibules, throne rooms and audience chambers of the great palaces; but it would be a mistake to see in them provision for a ceremonial that is not only anachronistic for the time of Diocletian but is inappropriate to what is known of his status and mode of life during retirement. It must be remembered in this respect that his only recorded activity was the growing of fine vegetables by his own hands.

The palace erected by Diocletian at Antioch on an island in the river Orontes is known mainly from a description by the orator Libanius.[151] The principal apartments of the palace within the walled city lay at the end of one of two intersecting streets, to form a monumental entrance, seemingly similar to the peristyle and great porch *(prothyron)* at Split. At Antioch also there was a great façade looking out over water with loggias in a colonnade. The similarity has also been noted between the porch at Split, with its raised arch above the central opening, and the façade on the silver dish *(missorium)* of Theodosius, which may be that of the Palace at Milan.[152] The 'ceremonial' interpretation is an elaboration of the 'palatial' interpretation and, as expounded by Ejnar Dyggve, detects a ceremonial complex of chambers along the central axis leading to an imperial throne-room.[153]

As Duval has explained in a paper of massive authority, these theories concerning the workings of Diocletian's villa were largely unfounded even before post-war excavations not only furnished a fuller understanding of how the various elements functioned, but removed some of the assumptions that lay behind earlier interpretations.[154] In this light one can set aside notions of Split's position in 'palatial' architecture: the evidence from elsewhere is too meagre, buildings erected at different periods and for different purposes are crudely juxtaposed, while some superficial similarities are overvalued.

Since the exceptional preservation of Split accords it an important place in the study of Late Roman architecture, it will be worthwhile to summarise Duval's refutation of the 'palatial' interpretations.

Little is known of late Roman palaces; nothing of Nicomedia where Diocletian ruled, more of Constantinople, though the remains are yet to be fully understood. The plan of the residence of Philip at his birthplace (Chahba) Philippopolis in Arabia has been traced but is yet to be explored and its relationship to the city is far from clear. Libanius tells us of the entrance and river façade of Antioch but nothing of its internal plan. As a consequence the exceptional remains at Split can lead to a circularity in argument. Like Antioch the palace of Galerius at Thessalonica was located in a city and furnishes no direct comparison with Split. Nevertheless its extensive remains are contemporary with Split and some of its components may offer suggestive comparison with parts of Split (e.g. the *triclinium* and the great octagon; see above p. 61 and n. 141). The palace was located on the east edge of the city and probably extended *c.* 800m inland from the sea shore. Its width was *c.* 200m. Surviving parts include an arch to commemorate Galerius' victory over the Persians, a rotunda, the octagon (perhaps the *triclinium)* and sections of the hippodrome.[155]

Its unique purpose makes Split incomparable. The villa for retirement was built in open country (Plate 19), while palaces were built in cities (Milan, Sirmium, Trier, etc.) and, compared with Antioch or Philippopolis, the area enclosed by the walls of Split is tiny. It is a fortified residence combining elements which are military, urban and those of a private villa. A good modern description is, as Duval suggests, 'chateau'.[156]

If one examines the specific features of Split cited for the 'palatial' interpretation, one is soon confronted with a confused application of the 'comparative method' in architectural studies. Its perimeter walls are not the defences of a city. The portico façade at Split is not the 'symbol of ruling authority' in a palace but a traditional façade, especially for a building overlooking water. Principal streets flanked by colonnades intersecting at a right-angle were a traditional Hellenistic arrangement which became common in cities of the eastern Roman provinces. Nothing can be adduced for Split from the fact that in the palaces at Thessalonica and Constantinople mausoleum and palace were linked by colonnaded streets.[157] The approach to the private apartments at Split through the peristyle does echo Libanius' description of Antioch, where the approach is by the shorter and more ornate street leading from the central intersection. But the entrance at Antioch is the external gate of the palace complex whereas at Split the porch and peristyle are internal entrances. The proper parallel, if one is to be sought, must be the external entrance on the same axis, that is the north gate.

The 'ceremonial' interpretation by E. Dyggve proposed a complex of buildings: an 'open-air basilica' or 'open-air audience chamber', a

Plate 19   Bird's-eye view of the palace (Hébrard-Zeiller)

monumental porch to serve as a frame for appearances of the ruler and a covered throne room directly behind this entrance. It is detected in the palace at Ravenna of the early sixth century and also at Split in the early fourth. The same arrangement is inferred for Constantinople from the Book of Ceremonies. The interpretation of the remains at Ravenna is far from certain[158] and nothing implied for Constantinople can be matched to the ordered arrangement suggested for Split. Now there is to hand conclusive evidence that the role of the peristyle and of the rooms aligned to it was for communication and not to serve as open-air basilicas or the like.

Even if one leaves aside the reasonable doubt that little if anything of the court ceremonial envisaged in the interpretation of Dyggve had actually existed by the early fourth century, the 'ceremonial' role of the peristyle remains doubtful.[159] In the time of Niemann great significance was attached to the fact that the cornice moulding of the great porch was continued around one of the sides and was later overlain by the attached architrave of the south arcade fronting the mausoleum *temenos*. It was suggested that the two precincts were secondary structures and that the areas north of the apartments either side of the peristyle were intended as open spaces.[160] At the time such a structural inconsistency appeared very significant but as many more have since been discovered in the remains, it now appears less exceptional. Moreover, the apparent imbalance between the congested mausoleum *temenos* and the barely filled temple *temenos,* also taken as a sign of changes, has now been corrected by the identification of two circular structures, probably temples, in its front corners.

The discovery of steps leading from the peristyle down to the basement chamber of the vestibule has had two results: it removes notions that the peristyle was solely an open court before the great porch and it shows that the lower paving of the area was part of a north–south axis which continued below the imperial apartments to the south gate. The fact that the walls of the underground aisled chamber represent a precise continuation of the peristyle colonnades emphasises a structural continuity that is concealed by the changes of level. The function of the peristyle was to relate the levels of the streets in the north half with the two levels in the south. The raising of the private apartments on basements had been made necessary to keep the south walls and façade at roughly the same level as the north walls. Had the peristyle been intended merely as an approach to the apartments there would have been no need to lower its level with the three surrounding steps. Whatever function the peristyle had served after its construction, it had not been created specifically as an 'open-air ceremonial basilica'.

The belief in a ceremonial function in the axial arrangement of the vestibule and triple-arched chamber on the south (so-called *tablinum)* has merely been modified to take account of recent discoveries in the peristyle.[161] One theory takes up the significance of the dome as a symbol of royal authority: as a result it is proposed that Split is a variety of the portico villa facing south. At the centre the aisled chamber was a reception hall leading to the throne room, i.e. the circular chamber now labelled vestibule. In a later consideration E. Dyggve modified his early view of ceremonial complex embracing the peristyle, but maintained that the great porch was the formal entrance, making the vestibule the antechamber and the three-aisled hall *(tablinum)* the throne room. Both interpretations stem from a wish to relate the plan of Split to wider notions of architectural symbolism, the nature and significance of the dome and the origins of Christian basilicas in the audience chamber of the *Palatium.* Neither furthers our understanding of Split and such notions have inevitably had to be adjusted to new discoveries in a fashion that hardly sustains their essential credibility.

THE 'MILITARY'INTERPRETATION

Some parts of the residence are reminiscent of late Roman military fortifications. The plan of the perimeter walls is that of a rectangular *castrum,* a type of fortification erected by the Tetrarchs and their successors around the frontiers of the empire. The arrangements at Split are unusual for the polygonal gate-towers being placed in their entirety in front of the perimeter wall. In plan the gates recall those of Augustan *coloniae* (including the so-called *porta Caesarea* at Salona) but the closest contemporary parallels are the late fortified centres in the interior of Pannonia. Here circular towers are set entirely beyond the perimeter wall and the available dating evidence indicates construction under the Tetrarchs or Constantine.[162] The perimeter walls have a patrol walk at the upper level, and the corner, interval and gate towers have windows which ostensibly permitted the use of artillery. The gates are single passage, with an inner and outer entrance separated by a court *(propugnaculum).* There is no evidence of any protective ditch or outwork in the vicinity. The enclosing walls present an appearance rather than the reality of a military fortification. Though obviously intended to ensure privacy and security, there is no suggestion that the walls of Split were ever intended to serve as military fortifications. Within the walls the perimeter buildings against the inside of the northern perimeter can be matched to those in late Roman forts. The arrangement of streets is a startling evocation of the classical military arrangement of *via praetoria* leading from the north gate (*porta praetoria*) to a junction with a *via principalis* between the east and west gates (*porta principalis dextra* and *sinistra*). In the traditional arrangement the centre of the fort opposite the road junction was occupied by the headquarters building (*principia*) flanked by the commander's residence (*praetorium*). It is tempting to seek some representation of these and in particular the shrine (*aedes*) of the standards, placed centrally at the rear of the classical principia. A 'military' interpretation of Split has recently been expounded by Rudolf Fellmann.[163]

By the end of the third century several variations existed from the traditional internal arrangements of a Roman military camp. The classical plan stemming from republican times placed *principia* at the centre opposite to the junction of the main streets. It remains in the forts on Hadrian's Wall and in legionary fortresses such as Carnuntum on the Danube. A second variety places all internal buildings against the inside of the perimeter walls, leaving most of the interior an open space. At least two forts of this type (in Arabia) are dated to the reign of Diocletian. A third arrangement appears to envisage removing the *principia* from its central place and a quartering of the interior by intersecting streets between gates placed centrally in the four sides. This is perhaps best represented in the late phase at Drobeta (Turnu-Severi) on the north bank of the Danube, where Trajan's bridge once spanned the river.[164] A fourth variation has the central intersection of principal streets with a headquarters block set against the rear of the interior opposite the principal gate, on the same axis as the approaching street. The type is best represented in the Diocletianic fortress in the western part of Palmyra, and its similarities to the plan of Split have long been recognised.[165] Some forts have a combination of these features in their internal arrangements: thus Da'ajaniya in Arabia has perimeter buildings and a centrally located *principia*, a *via principalis* and the rest of the interior occupied with barracks but with no *porta* or *via praetoria*.[166] The late fort at Dionysias in Egypt has perimeter buildings, with the *principia* at the end of a colonnaded street on a central axis from the single gate. On either side of the street are open courts flanked by porticos.[167]

A consistent feature of late-Roman forts is the disappearance of the clear differentiation between administrative headquarters (*principia)* and commander's residence (*praetorium*). At Dionysias the two appear to be combined in a single block. In the forts of Hadrian's Wall there is evidence for alteration of parts of the traditional *principia* as dwelling quarters. In newly constructed forts of the late period, the headquarters loses its traditional courtyard and aisled hall (cross-hall) behind which lay a row of small rooms with the 'chapel of the standards' (*aedes*) at the centre. By the fourth century there was a concentration on the shrine, now more the centre of emperor worship. The *principia* of third-century Drobeta (Turnu-Severin)[168] is an aisled hall that continues the axis of the *via praetoria* to end in an enlarged shrine. The old court and cross-hall and flanking rooms have all disappeared. At Dionysias the shrine is the central feature with steps leading up to its raised podium from the colonnaded street.

At Split the intersecting colonnaded streets (that included the basement street from peristyle to south gate), the perimeter buildings (though now known to be confined to the northern half), the buildings in the northern interior and the intervallum road are elements of contemporary military architecture, albeit in unique combination. There remains the question of whether one can identify in the southern half the elements of a *principia* as it had developed in military architecture. The façade of the great porch has a striking similarity to that of the *aedes* in the classical *principia*. The tripartite division with a raised arch above the central opening appears first on the hilt of the famous sword of Tiberius, from the time of Augustus, and (inferred from plans) in Flavian legionary fortresses at Vindonissa and Vetera as the façade of the *aedes principiorum*.[169] The parallel becomes valid as the peristyle is placed on the classical site of the *principia* and, like that of Drobeta, forms a colonnaded approach (here open) leading to the *aedes*. It is nevertheless also possible to regard the whole residential block, including the vestibule and porch, as representing a *principia* set against the perimeter wall opposite the principal entrance (here north gate) and approached by the short and more ornate arm leading from the intersection of the streets.

The military parallels appear valid and instructive, especially so in the light of new discoveries, both at Split and in late forts on the eastern frontiers. The military significance of peristyle, porch and vestibule is intelligible as a provision for military ceremony implied by the arrangement in contemporary forts. These buildings lie on a central axis as did the classical *principia* and its *aedes signorum*. Like the *praetorium*, Diocletian's private residence lay alongside the military shrine. It conveys an image of the elderly Diocletian emerging from his seclusion to receive at the *aedes* a facsimile of an acclamation due to one who still retained the dignity of an Augustus.

THE 'CHÂTEAU' OF DIOCLETIAN

The fuller understanding of the nature and function of the peristyle following the excavations of Marasović is crucial to our understanding of the residence as a whole. This applies especially to the matter of the relationship between the residential block and the rest of the interior.[170] Its lowered floor level served to link both the raised floor of this block and its basement *c.* 8m lower with the ground level in the rest of the interior. For this it had to combine the role of continuing the axial street with a combination of entrance to the apartments and a continuation of the street below to the south gate. What remains uncertain is whether the flanking colonnades were part of an original design or perhaps the result of trial and error over a number of years. In its finished state the peristyle may have been the scene of elaborate ceremonials but these were not the purpose for which it had been created.

The 'ceremonial' role of the vestibule has been especially prominent in the interpretation of Split. The chamber below is now revealed to be cruciform, astride an intersection between the north–south axial street and not another street but entrances to courtyards on either side probably leading to the East and West Baths. If one regards the upper chamber with a conviction that the dome is a symbol of sovereignty it is then possible to imagine the chamber as a throne room. But the vestibule has entrances on the north and south and four niches set diagonally, an arrangement hardly suggestive of a throne room. There is just no warrant for seeing at Split a precursor to the throne rooms and domes of later eras. The vestibule is in all probability correctly identified by its traditional name. It is a vestibule, an entrance chamber at the line of entry to a block that is aligned on a different axis.[171]

Behind the vestibule the large rectangular chamber (*c.* 31 by 12m) has attracted attention. Since the time of Niemann and Hébrard-Zeiller it has been labelled the *tablinum,* the principal central chamber of Italian *atrium* houses opposite the entrance. Save for the narrow service passages, this chamber is the sole means of entering the residence from the rest of the interior. It may have been an imposing and highly decorated chamber but its function as a means of entrance is sufficient to rule out notions of throne-room or the like, for which there is no material evidence. It is reasonable to follow Duval's conclusion that this chamber did not delay those entering the apartments and the true reception room or rooms are to be sought elsewhere.[172]

The principal room of the private apartments is the three-aisled basilica (no. 6) whose central axis is marked by the raised arch and wider opening in the south façade. The presence of the apse, the three symmetrically placed entrances from the gallery, and two entrances in each of the sides, which crossed the light-wells on either side of the chamber, are together suggestive of a formal public room. Both Niemann and Hébrard had suggested that the chamber was a library. Yet if one discards ceremonial notions for the rooms on the central axis this hall can be seen as the principal chamber in the whole residence. It is the basilica in a private residence and its function was that of a reception room, of a type well known in the late Empire. No liturgies need be invoked for the presence of a chamber that is an accepted element in the private residence for a person of the highest class.[173]

The private dwelling block is composed of three elements, entrance chambers on the central axis, private apartments, including audience chamber in the west, and dining room *(triclinium)* in the east, both opening off the long gallery. The rooms on the central axis are no more than a continuation of the principal circulation route. The principal audience chamber is set apart from this, alongside and facing in the opposite direction. The north–south axis was combined with that from east to west, dictated by the great façade facing the sea. The elements of the traditional peristyle residence are adapted to the

Plate 20   Mosaic with *villa* of Julius Dominus at Carthage.

73

Plate 21   *Villa urbana* in central apse mosaic at Tabarka.

positioning of the two monumental façades, that of entrance on the north facing the peristyle and that of the opened-out peristyle in the gallery through which all the private rooms faced the sea.

The south façade of Split is perhaps the best-preserved example of a 'portico-villa with flanking corner-towers'. The most instructive parallel to Split in this respect is the villa at Nennig in the Mosel valley 40km upstream from Trier.[174] Its porticoed façade is flanked by two tower-like wings. What is especially significant is that, behind the two storeys of the façade portico, the rooms of the main residential block are grouped around an internal peristyle court and the whole scheme converges upon a central *triclinium*. Behind the 77m colonnade a vestibule led to a large hall at the centre of the block, with a fountain. On the north was a peristyle with swimming pool and *tablinum* behind. On the other side of the hall lay a suite of rooms, some of which had hypocaust heating. The whole residence was embellished with mosaic floors, painted walls and stucco mouldings. The principal difference from Split is that the main entrance was in the middle of the façade. Were it from the north the circulation system of Nennig would differ little from Split.

Several villas portrayed on late-Roman mosaics in North Africa have a number of features in common with the south façade of Split. That depicted on a late-fourth century mosaic from Carthage (Plate 20), where its owner is named Dominus Julius, has at the upper level an arcade across the full width of the façade between two towers with pointed roofs and windows at the upper level in each storey.[175] At ground floor level the wall is plain masonry, broken only by a central doorway and doors into the towers. Behind the façade rises the pitched roof and walls of a large chamber, with windows at the upper level. Alongside this a group of buildings shown with domed roofs which may be identified as baths. Though the villa faces a rural landscape and not water the similarity with Split is striking. Around the villa are shown a variety of activities appropriate to a large country estate. It need not be doubted that this is an actual residence, the central image of a floor laid in the town residence to remind its owners of their life in the country. Certainly villas of this type do appear as a background detail to the scenes of hunting popular on floor mosaics of the upper classes at this era,[176] and they are perhaps unlikely to be realistic portrayals of actual buildings. At the same time they do show that the common idea of the country residence was enclosed by high plain walls, with single entrances at ground level, loggias, galleries and windows at the upper level, and towers at the sides or corners (Plate 21). One can be certain that Split, seen from the sea, will have been instantly recognisable as the country residence of a prominent person. Indeed it may well have inspired those who saw it to an emulation on their own land.

It is tempting to entertain the notion that such was the case with the much debated fortified residence at Mogorjelo in the Neretva valley, around 150km along the coast south of Split. It lies alongside the river near modern Čapljina 20km inland and may be identified with a place *Ad Turres* named on the Peutinger Map on the road between Narona and Diluntum.[177] A modest *villa rustica* of the first century AD was replaced around the end of the third century by a large residence set within a walled precinct (92 by 75m) with towers at the corners (Fig. 10).[178] The three gates are also flanked by towers, and on the south-west wall, where there was no gate, a single tower was attached to the wall. Against the inside of the north-west and northeast walls, and half of the south-east wall were perimeter buildings, rows of chambers 4m square each with a single entrance. These were fronted by a corridor behind an arcade between the north-east and south-east gates. The residential block occupied the south-west half of the interior. The remainder of the interior was an open court formed by the perimeter arcade. Here were a large

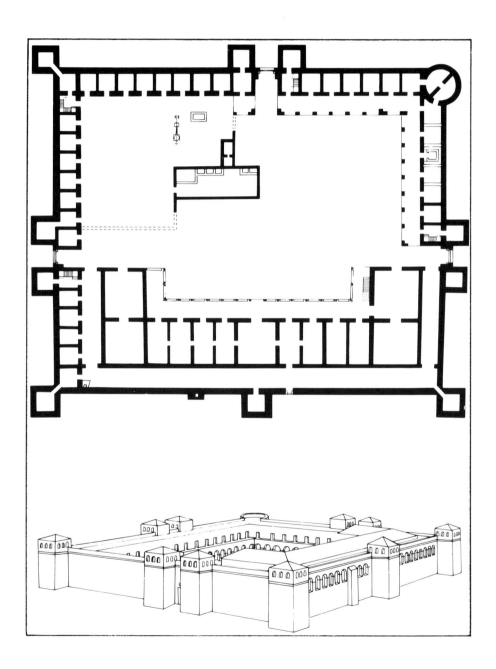

Figure 10 Plan and reconstruction of villa at Mogorjelo by E. Dyggve.

press, a store with *dolia* set in the floor and two rooms with hypocaust heating (incorporated from an earlier building).

The residential block is a portico-villa with wings projecting towards the interior. An imaginative reconstruction by Dyggve has suggested that there was an upper storey, fronted on the outer (south-west) side by an arcade above the perimeter wall. It would be an attractive and intriguing analogy with Split, if only there was any evidence from the site to support this reconstruction.[179] The building had evidently ceased to function properly by the fifth century, by which time twin Christian basilicas were erected above the south end of the residence. It lies at the heart of one of the most fertile areas of Dalmatia and must have been the working centre of an estate. The apparently sudden construction of such a complex invites comparison with Split, since it was erected at around the same date. Conceivably, Mogorjelo, though around 100 miles away, was an imperial property where the operations of a large rural establishment were concentrated to support the new residence at Split. It is likely that the needs of that establishment, foodstuffs, equipment, etc., may have demanded a working estate elsewhere in the area. Diocletian's fine vegetables and other produce will hardly have sufficed for his entire household.

ROMULIANA (GAMZIGRAD): RESIDENCE OF GALERIUS

Until a few years ago the villa of Piazza Armerina in central Sicily would have been presented as the closest and most authentic companion to Split, since it had been identified as the retirement residence of Diocletian's colleague, Maximian. Until recently less attention, if any, would have been given to the fortified site of Gamzigrad in the remote hills of eastern Serbia. Now the imperial title to the Sicilian retreat has been challenged with powerful arguments, while an inscription has recently revealed that Gamzigrad is Romuliana, Galerius' place of burial in his native Dacia Ripensis, named after his formidable mother Romula.

Piazza Armerina is a sprawling complex of linked vestibules, corridors, peristyle courts, audience chambers and suites of private rooms.[180] It is best known for its astonishing collection of figured mosaics in a variety of colours, most likely the work of craftsmen from North Africa. Even if it had been well-founded, the notion that such an architectural fantasy, where one might expect to meet the like of Hadrian or perhaps the Younger Pliny, was the chosen retreat for retirement of Diocletian's loyal colleague, Maximian (or perhaps his son Maxentius), who hailed from humble origins in the Middle Danube lands, was hard to credit. The contrast with the compact and disciplined order of Diocletian's residence could not be greater. The arguments for imperial ownership, advanced when the discovery of the villa was a recent sensation, rest both on ornament and on architectural form, the triple-arched entrance and the great audience chamber, and the use of 'imperial' porphyry in the apse of the hall. To this was added a judgement that the Proconnesian capitals were newly-produced in the same workshop at the same time as those of Split.[181] In the mosaics the similarity of a flat-topped beret to that worn by the Venice Tetrarchs was held to be significant. Moreover, Maximian himself, it was claimed, could be recognised among the figures. A later hypothesis introduced Maxentius, the son of Maximian, as a possible proprietor and he too was alleged to be identifiable with one of the figures in the mosaics. These and other arguments demanded that the villa be constructed around the time of Maximian's retirement (305) and certainly before the final rupture between him and Maxentius (308). Against this, limited evidence from the site would appear to make it more likely that construction began not before the beginning of the fourth century, and probably not before the second decade of the fourth century, thereby in all probability ruling out even the existence of the villa at the time of the First or Second Tetrarchy.[182]

The recently reported discovery of a monumental pediment inscribed FELIX ROMULIANA within a wreath has confirmed the identification of the remains at Gamzigrad near Zaječar with the burial place of Galerius in his native Dacia Ripensis. This discovery, along with the results of excavations within the defended perimeter, adds much to our understanding of the site's complicated history (Figure 11).[183] It now seems certain that one or both of its palatial residences was built for Galerius, perhaps a retreat for retirement if he should emulate the abdication of his former Augustus once he had passed his *vicennalia* in 313.[184] He died two years before that anniversary and in the event was buried at Romuliana.

Gamzigrad was evidently already inhabited in prehistoric times and may have been a settlement of the Triballi, a Thracian people known as troublesome neighbours of the Macedonians. During the second quarter of the third century AD the site was occupied by a corridor- or portico-villa, which has been compared with that at Mogorjelo in Dalmatia (see above p. 75). Around the end of the third century an imperial residence was erected on the site, of which the principal elements (as known in 1983) are the following:

(a) A fortified enclosure, similar in scale and construction to that of Split. The excavated West Gate has wholly projecting polygonal towers, and a section of the west wall square interval towers and an internal perimeter portico. The original plan, a rectangle 240 x 190m, evidently had to be modified because of the terrain to an irregular, roughly quadrilateral enclosure.

(b) A second phase of massive fortifications, erected outside the earlier defences (10.95m away). On the west a gate (located 8m farther south) with polygonal towers projecting entirely, and a perimeter wall with interior portico have been excavated. The monumental perimeter wall (3.65m thick) has great polygonal towers against its outer side, those at the corners being 30m in diameter. East and west walls are *c.* 200m and north and south *c.* 240m long, containing an area of *c.* 15 acres (*c.* 6ha). The new defences on the east were, through the slope of the ground, *c.* 9m higher than those on the west and contained the main entrance to the residence.

(c) A palatial residence (Palace 1) occupied an area in the north-west *c.* 50m square. At the centre was a large hall with apse and raised floor at the east end. It has been labelled 'audience chamber' and an octagonal room alongside, the 'robing room'. Two corridors led to the hall from the principal entrance at the south-east corner. On the north lay two peristyle courts, with marble columns, and another large chamber with an apse, identified as the dining room *(triclinium)*. Across one of the courts from the dining hall lay a small suite of baths, one circular room, one trefoil and another quatrefoil. The building had rich decoration. The south and west walls were covered with coloured marbles, serpentine and porphyry, and with marble pilasters. Interior surfaces had marble veneer on the lower parts, marked off from paintings on the upper surfaces by stucco mouldings. The vestibule or corridor west of the audience chamber has a mosaic floor with a geometric design confined by octagonal fields. The floor of the room opening off the vestibule on the south side of the building has a hexagonal *trompe l'oeil,* with city gates at the angles linked by crenellated perimeter walls. The 'audience chamber' has geometric mosaics along the sides and at the centre a fine panel of hunters and panthers within a guilloche border. In the large apsed hall the mosaic includes two figured panels, one of Dionysus. The peristyle corridors and the baths were both embellished with geometric floor mosaics.

(d) A small classical temple in the north, immediately east of the Palace I baths. It was Corinthian tetrastyle prostyle (16.5m by 10.5m), of which only the core of the podium, part of the crypt, foundations of porch and *cella* and a

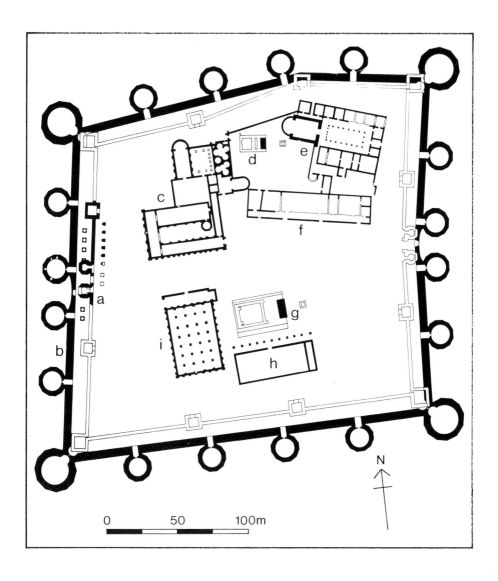

Figure 11   Plan of Gamzigrad, based on D. Srejović, D Janković, A. Lalović and V
Jović, *Gamzigrad Kasnoantički Carski Dvorac* (Belgrade, 1983), figs 19–21.
Drawn by David Price.

large altar are preserved. The cruciform crypt with a basin has been identified as the pit *(fossa sanguinis),* associated with the *taurobulium* rite in the cult of Cybele.

(e) A second palatial complex (Palace II), as yet not fully excavated. Its three principal elements comprise: 1) a central complex of a large apsed hall, two other rooms and a peristyle; 2) a north wing comprising an entrance corridor and eight rooms and 3) a south wing with a gate, two rooms, a garden, an antechamber and five rectangular rooms.

(f) South of Palace II lies a rectangular building 80 by 18m, divided into a narrow corridor and several rooms of unequal dimensions.

(g) At the centre of the southern half of the interior lay the massive foundations of a temple 32.60m by 23.80m. The podium 4.5m high of limestone blocks contains a double crypt. The *cella* was 15.25 by 11.50m, with *antae* forming a shallow antechamber. Marble sculptures of several deities, notably Hercules and emperors in military dress, have been discovered near the temple.

(h) South of the temple lay a rectangular building (51.20 by 19.40m) on a similar alignment. It was erected on the remains of the earlier villa (see above p. 79) and consisted of a large hall and small antechamber. On the north a row of pillars formed a porch along one of the long sides.

(i) Finally a large rectangular (15.20 by 19.40m) building, probably for storage *(horrea)* with 24 supports (in four rows) for the upper floor. The entrance lay on the north side within a porch formed by a row of pillars. A similar building, evidently for grain storage (44 by 16m) and contemporary with the later fortifications was found 300m to the south-west.

The certain identification with Romuliana (-um) and the increasing dating-evidence recovered by excavation permit the two principal phases to be linked with the career of Galerius. The earlier phase of fortifications (a, above) and perhaps the temple of Cybele (d, above) belong to the period when as Caesar (from AD 293) Galerius began to embellish his birthplace now renamed after his mother Romula.[185] As Augustus after 305 he could contemplate his own retirement and sought to emulate his old chief by erecting a palatial complex within monumental protective walls.[186] In the event the 'palatial' phase was brief. Work may have been continued under the rule of Licinius after 311 but hardly after 314 when he lost control of Dacia Ripensis. Gamzigrad continued to be occupied until the seventh century (though it evidently suffered from the presence in the area of the Huns), and was resettled by the Byzantines for a few decades in the eleventh century after the capture of Vidin nearby on the

Danube. Unlike Split, Gamzigrad shows only deserted ruins from those few years when it also was intended as the safe retreat of a retired Augustus. The historical and archaeological importance of its remains, so closely dated, is great. When fully excavated and studied it may furnish vital evidence not only for understanding the residence of Diocletian but for the early development of late Roman architecture.

CHAPTER 5

THE FATE OF DIOCLETIAN'S VILLA

FROM DIOCLETIAN'S DEATH TO THE COMING OF THE SLAVS

The province of Dalmatia was little affected by Diocletian's reorganisation of provinces. Throughout the fourth century it continued to be administered by a governor (*praeses*) resident at Salona and belonged to the Diocese of Illyricum that formed part of the western empire.[187] It suffered little from either civil wars or foreign invasions during the fourth and fifth centuries. The military collapse of the Rhine and Danube frontiers during the early years of Honorius (395–423) had its effect upon the northern part of Dalmatia but it seems hardly at all upon the Adriatic coast. Indeed it became a haven for refugees of all classes and even whole state institutions were removed there from the middle Danube provinces.[188] Dalmatia passed to the eastern empire following the accession of Valentinian III at Ravenna in 425. The little that is known of its history from then until it passed under the Ostrogoths in 493 points to something approaching independence under local rulers.[189]

Of the fate of Diocletian's residence during this time almost nothing is recorded. The story of a plot under Constantius II (in 356/7) to steal the purple robe from the tomb does imply that the mausoleum and its contents were intact, and it seems that they remained so during the fifth century also.[190] What Diocletian had devised for his privacy could easily be adapted to function as a means of imprisonment. In the 360s and 370s there are stories of exiles being despatched to Dalmatia but only to the bleak offshore island of Čiovo (ancient Boa or Bua), which adjoins the mainland at Trogir.[191] It appears that the villa contained a large resident population, from the evidence of a cemetery outside the North Wall dating to the sixth century.[192]

By this time at least part of Diocletian's residence had been adapted to serve as a state textile or clothing factory. Nothing is known of the nature or scale of its operations: its presence will have made it impossible to maintain the servicing of the apartments to the level enjoyed by Diocletian, but a princely villa may still have remained intact for the occasional noble resident, willing or otherwise. The latter applies to the sojourn of Galla Placidia Augusta, daughter of Theodosius I, who stayed at Salona, probably in Diocletian's villa, along with her son Valentinian before they left to claim the throne at Ravenna in 425.[193]

The death in 454 of the mighty Aetius, the great general and minister of Valentinian III, appears to have provoked an assertion of independence by Marcellinus, military Count of Dalmatia and a supporter of Aetius. Until he was murdered during a campaign in Sicily in 468, Marcellinus, a devout pagan, maintained what amounted to an independent power in Dalmatia, through good administration and an efficient military and naval organisation.[194] Most likely he resided in Diocletian's residence (as his nephew Nepos evidently did). Behind Marcellinus there must lie a support of major local families and other interests which combined to form a base in Dalmatia that was virtually impregnable. In 474 Julius Nepos, nephew of Marcellinus and heir to his power, expelled the emperor Glycerius, proclaimed only in March the previous year, and assumed the throne at Ravenna. His predecessor was removed to Salona and was almost immediately consecrated its bishop. When Nepos himself fled from Ravenna on 28th August 475 he returned to the safety of Salona. He maintained his power there for another five years, asserting on coins his legal title as Augustus in the west.[195] Once he sought to gain the assistance of the emperor Zeno to regain the throne from the usurper Odovacar. On the 9th May 480 Nepos was murdered in his villa 'not far from Salona', presumably Spalato. The perpetrators were his followers Viator and Ovida (or Odiva), though one account implicates Glycerius, still bishop at Salona. Ovida's attempt to maintain an independent power in Dalmatia was swiftly ended by Odovacar.[196] During the sixty or so years of Ostrogothic rule, most of which appear to have been peaceful, the residence may have been used by the Count who controlled Dalmatia. The Roman administration, including taxation, mines, estates and factories, was retained.[197] In 537 the Goths were driven out of Dalmatia in an operation preliminary to the recovery of Italy by the Byzantine Empire. By now the Avars and Slavs were moving south-west from the middle Danube and before the end of the sixth century they were raiding the coast. Salona fell, or rather was abandoned, in the early seventh century.[198] The future now lay, as some may already have guessed, within the security of the *villa* three miles away. Salona was to remain in ruins. Now begins the history of medieval and modern Split.

THE ORIGINS OF SPLIT [199]

An account of the history of the Salona Church was compiled by Thomas the Archdeacon. Born in 1200, as a student he heard St Francis preach in Bologna and was much moved by his talent to reconcile enemies. Returning to Split he was made canon but his zeal for reform provoked hostility. He attacked the laxity of the archbishop and won a notable victory in a hearing before Pope Gregory IX at Perugia. He was successful in securing election of an Italian *podesta* to ensure efficient and impartial administration in Split. Thomas gives a vivid account of the Tartar invasion of Dalmatia of 1241–2, when Split and others withstood demands to hand over the king of Hungary. Gifted and respected, Thomas appears to have been denied the highest office through numerous quarrels with laity and other churchmen. He died in 1268. [200]

According to Thomas, the *Romani* of Salona fled first to the islands where they suffered a miserable existence. Their young men made boats and raided the mainland to drive the Slavs away from the coast. A leading exile named Severus encouraged the fugitives to return to the mainland, not to Salona but to the villa of Diocletian on the coast, where they could remain until Salona was liberated. His own residence was 'a house that stood next to the columns of the palace by the sea'. [201] Other leading citizens were encouraged to inhabit the better parts while the poor took over the towers and the basements. The barbarians attacked the new settlement and the lands surrounding. Eventually the *Romani* were confirmed in possession of their new settlement by the emperor and the newcomers were told to cease their attacks. From then the two communities began a co-existence in peace and harmony. The bishopric was re-established at Split with the election of the papal legate, John of Ravenna. In 650 the 'Temple of Jupiter' (in fact the mausoleum) was cleared of its pagan idols and dedicated to the 'honour of God and the glorious Virgin Mary'. [202] An expedition was sent to Salona to retrieve the relics of St Domnius. The searchers, confronted by overgrown ruins and fearful of the Slavs, brought back the wrong coffin but a second expedition found the right saint and placed his remains in the new cathedral. For the thirteenth century the point of this version was to support the claim of Split to all the authority of the ancient archbishops of Salona, that is primacy over all Dalmatia.

Domnius (or Domnio) was martyred under Diocletian on 10th April 304 in the amphitheatre at Salona. [203] He, another priest Asterius and four soldiers, were buried in a martyr's shrine close by (Kapljuč). Around the same time Anastasius, a fuller from Aquileia, was martyred and interred in a burial at Marusinac, north of the city. The Salona church evidently prospered during the fourth century. In the fifth century its bishops may have received archiepiscopal status and were prominent in the attacks on Arianism. By the late sixth century the church was in decline. There was strife between the 'western' interests supported by Pope Gregory I and the imperial party. The last known archbishop was Maximus, champion of the imperial party, who was eventually reconciled with Gregory. Only two names appear after his in the list of bishops, the last recorded fleeing to Italy.[204]

The papal chronicle records, in 641, what appears as the last episode in the history of the Salona church. In that year the Dalmatian Pope John IV negotiated the recovery of the relics of the Salona martyrs from the Slavs. They were brought to Rome and the saints were portrayed in wall mosaic in the chapel of St Venantius in the Lateran.[205] Both the date and the authenticity of John of Ravenna's renewal of the Salona church have been doubted. Some have dated the episode to the end of the eighth century and have placed it in the context of Charlemagne's conquest of the Dalmatian Slavs.[206] That does not deny the account of a population maintaining itself in the villa in the face of Slav invaders as early seventh century. Though several have asserted a continuity of occupation throughout this period, no material evidence can be produced to support it (see below). A catalogue of remains that may be dated before 800 is a brief one.[207] The St John's Cross incised on the arch of the West Gate, in place of a winged Victoria, could be dated to the fifth or sixth century from similar crosses on sarcophagi at Ravenna. The same date can be suggested for two crosses incised on pilasters discovered in remains behind the mausoleum *temenos*. The column and Corinthian capital adjoining a house near the temple have been dated to the fifth or sixth century.[208] Nearby also an ornate arcade in the corner of a house is dated to the seventh or eighth centuries from parallels in North Africa.

In what is now the Split baptistery (formerly the classical temple) has long stood the sarcophagus of Archbishop John.[209] One theory discards the story of archbishop John of Ravenna in the mid-seventh century (as given by Thomas the Archdeacon) but suggests that there was still such a person and that he was active a century or more later. It is unlikely that relics removed to Rome under Pope John IV (AD 640–2) were somehow back in Dalmatia and in the cathedral of Split only ten years later. The sarcophagus and epitaph may be dated to the end of the eighth century and very likely does belong to John of Ravenna. His tenure may be dated to the time when Frankish missionaries were active among the Croatian Slavs after the victory of Charlemagne, *c.* 800, that is between the revival of the Split church and the re-establishment of Byzantine rule in Dalmatia. This took place probably when the emperor Basil I forced the Arabs to abandon the siege of Ragusa (Dubrovnik) in 868. At this time also relations between the cities of the Dalmatian *Theme* and the Slavs appear to have been put on a more settled basis.[210] It is from the following century that we have the first reliable description of Split (Spalato), the city built within the walls of Diocletian's *villa:*

'The city of Spalato, which means 'little palace' was founded by the emperor Diocletian; he made it his own dwelling-place, and built within it a court and a palace, most part of which has been destroyed. But a few things remain to this day, e.g. the episcopal residence of the city and the church of St Domnus, in which lies St Domnus himself, and which was the resting-place of the same emperor Diocletian. Beneath it are arching vaults, which used to be prisons, in which he cruelly confined the saints whom he tormented. St Anastasius also lies in this city.

The defence wall of this city is constructed neither of bricks nor of concrete, but of ashlar blocks, one and often two fathoms in length by a fathom across, and these are fitted and joined to one another by iron cramps puddled into molten lead. In this city also stand close rows of columns, with entablatures above, on which this same emperor Diocletian proposed to erect arching vaults, to a height of two and three stories, so that they covered little ground-space in the same city. The defence wall of this city has neither rampart nor bulwarks, but only lofty walls and arrow-slits'

(Constantine Porphyrogenitus, De Administrando Imperii
c. 29, 237–57, translated R.J.H. Jenkins).

This account by the Byzantine emperor was probably composed in AD 948–9 and attests that what had been the imperial villa was now an established city.[211] It gives some indication of how much of the original building had been destroyed. The 'rows of columns, with entablatures above', on which Diocletian was supposed to have planned to erect covering vaults, were evidently the still surviving colonnades flanking the principal streets.

Something of the stages by which this transformation came about can be understood from recent excavation, where it has been possible to examine some stratified deposits.[212] Little change can be detected for the three centuries after Diocletian. No structures of the Roman period which are demonstrably secondary to Diocletianic arrangements can be cited. Roman pottery and a least one later floor using Roman material indicates habitation but nothing of its nature. The contrast with Salona, where several major buildings, including churches and martyrs' shrines, were erected is striking. A few fragments of architecture may derive from buildings of this era since they are unlikely to have come from outside.[213] The residence may already have been occupied by refugees in the sixth century and it is possible that the fall of Salona did no more than enlarge an existing settlement. Late Roman pottery, including wine and oil amphorae, ceased to be introduced after the sixth century and so provides no evidence for any continuity of external contacts though its absence does not rule out a continuity of occupation. Perhaps it is best to remain with the belief that it is inconceivable such a place could ever have been wholly derelict, except in the immediate aftermath of catastrophe (sacking or plague).

The first post-Roman structures are fragile walls, made of rough stones packed in a yellow clay, in the spaces between standing Roman buildings. They formed small chambers and cannot have risen above single-storey level. Their dating remains a problem, though a group of them built over the *palaestra* of the east baths had apparently already been partly demolished when burials were laid over them in the tenth century.[214] That aside, it does appear that these buildings are the remains of the city described by Constantine. The pottery of the period between the seventh and the eleventh century — as far as it can be identified — appears to consist entirely of local wares. In firing and making it is markedly inferior to imported wares of the earlier period and the closest parallels are with pottery from cemeteries elsewhere in Dalmatia labelled as 'slavic' ware.[215]

Until the twelfth century, when the medieval city as it exists today began to be created (Plate 22), within the walls much of the original Diocletianic fabric may have remained intact. Buildings were merely attached to standing walls of the fourth century rather than built over them. The material evidence for Spalato as portrayed by Constantine is meagre, but there are signs that it was no longer merely a settlement of refugee *Romani*. At the north gate, in the narrow passage within the wall on the north side of the courtyard, the chapel of St Martin has an altar-screen of the ninth century, in the style of those erected by Croatian rulers and nobles in the area of Split during the ninth and tenth centuries.[216] It is a significant pointer to the Slav

Plate 22   Aerial view of Split in 1920s. *Photo: Bulic-Karaman*, pl.26.

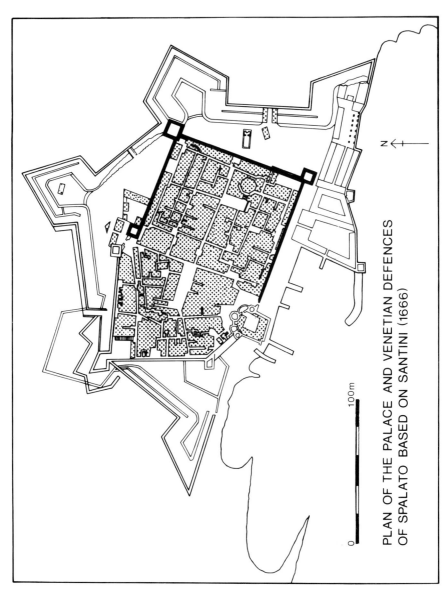

PLAN OF THE PALACE AND VENETIAN DEFENCES
OF SPALATO BASED ON SANTINI (1666)

Figure 12 Plan of Split and Venetian defences based on G. Santini, *Diverse vedute di Citta' di Dalmazia fatte l'Anno 1666.*

element in the population of Split. The recent discovery that Archbishop John, a native of Split of the early tenth century in the time of the Croatian King Tomislav, had a father whose first name was Tordacatus or Tvrtko in its Slav form, is a startling confirmation of the Slav element in the Split population at this time.[217]

Today one sees in Split the remains of a city created in the Middle Ages which survived centuries of neglect in the later years of Venetian rule (after 1420), when it was enclosed by a perimeter of massive defences devised for the era of gunpowder (Figure 12). Its heart is still the shell of Diocletian's residence, whose remains have become more exposed through clearance and restoration since the Second World War. The oldest surviving structure after the Roman period is the belfry at the west gate, erected over existing Roman walls *c.* 1100 for the chapel known as Our Lady of the Bells (Gospa od Zvonika).[218] In the twelfth and thirteenth centuries the elegant courtyard houses with three or more storeys in the Gothic style began to appear. Though they incorporated standing Roman structures they were not dictated by them, but now determine the pattern of narrow streets which still exist in the northern half of the interior.[219] They used dressed stones set in mortar and such buildings rapidly caused the infilling of any open spaces. No brick or roof tile was evidently available locally. Roman Dalmatia had imported these from north-east Italy, though a local factory produced the bricks for Diocletian's *villa*.[220] The trade was not revived until late in the Venetian period. By the thirteenth century the walls of Diocletian's villa, though still the main defence of Split, no longer confined the extent of its buildings. A new civic centre developed outside the walls on the west and by the end of the Middle Ages Split occupied an area more than twice that of Diocletian's residence.[221] With the Renaissance, when Split was the residence of several leading writers and scholars, began the rediscovery of Diocletian's *villa,* a process which was to prove so influential for the classical revival in European architecture.

REDISCOVERY OF 'DIOCLETIAN'S PALACE'

The first account of Diocletian's Palace we owe to Cyriac of Ancona, who travelled through Greece and Asia Minor in the middle of the fifteenth century. His main interest was the texts of ancient inscriptions. Returning to Venice from Achaea and Epirus he stopped in Dalmatia to copy inscriptions and on the 29th and 30th July 1436 he was at Spalato and Salona. 'The Palace built by Caesar Diocletian is called by its inhabitants today Spalatum.

The walls of this magnificent building serve as the defences of the city. At the centre stands the imposing Temple of Jupiter, which the citizens now use for the worship of the blessed priest Doimus.'[222]

The earliest local account, and the first written in Croatian, was by Marko Markulić (1450–1524) around the end of the fifteenth century. He describes the Temple of Jupiter and the 'Rotunda' (vestibule) where he reports traces of mosaic still in position. In 1567 Antonio Proculiano, born in Antivari (Bar) and Chancellor of the Split Commune, describes the Palace in an address delivered to the Rector. His account of the principal buildings appears to include a reference to the two recently discovered small circular structures in the corners of the temple temenos that have been identified as temples (see above p. 55). A work published in 1628 by Tomko Marnavić, a native of Šibenik and a bishop in Bosnia, tells the well known story that the porphyry sarcophagus of Diocletian was discovered in the south-east tower.[223]

The first known drawings are two plans of the mausoleum made by an Italian in the sixteenth century. When first recognized by Hébrard they were identified as the work of the renowned architect Andrea Palladio, born at Padua in 1508. It appears now that they were owned and annotated rather than created by him.[224] The first attempts at reconstruction of the palace as a whole were rather inexpert drawings published by Jakob Spon, doctor and antiquary of Lyon, and George Wheler of London, in their respective published accounts of their travels together in Italy and elsewhere. The perimeter is schematic, save for the west gate, which can be recognised, though part of the west façade is shown with the gallery of the south wall. Their account first drew the remains to the attention of French and English antiquaries.[225]

The first measured drawings of the palace were presented to the public by the Austrian architect of the late baroque, J.B. Fischer von Erlach, in his *Sketch of Historical Architecture* published in 1721 (Plate 23). For all their imaginative reconstruction, the drawings are based on measurements of the remains, made with the help of a collaborator in Split. His portrayal was adopted by Daniel Farlati for his monumental work *Illyricum Sacrum,* also with the aid of local antiquaries in Split.[226]

'The view of Spalato from the sea is not only picturesque but magnificent. Nor is this impression at all diminished by a nearer approach. So soon as you enter between the two points that jut out into the sea, forming a grand basin and commodious harbour, the remains of the massive wall and long arcade of the Emperor's Palace, the modern fortifications, the lazzaretto and towers within the walls, with one of the ancient temples, immediately present themselves to your view, all of which group so perfectly with the hills and the country around that they form a most agreeable landscape.'

So wrote Robert Adam of his first sight of Spalato in July 1757.[227] He had left Rome for the last time in May and travelled to Padua. From there he made a leisurely progress down the Brenta canal to admire the villas of the great Palladio. In Venice he prepared his expedition to Dalmatia to produce a book of drawings of the remains of Diocletian's Palace, complementing his earlier studies of the Baths of Diocletian at Rome. He had dreamed of Greece and even Egypt and the Holy Land but had neither time nor money for such ambitious expeditions. He had set out from Venice on 11th July with the French painter and architect C.L. Clérisseau and other draughtsmen. Though he had not secured the special permission needed to study what was still a fortified Venetian garrison, he felt especially confident knowing that an old friend and fellow-Scot, William Graeme of Bucklivie, was Commander-in-Chief of Venetian forces and due to inspect the garrison at Spalato. His welcome from the Commander-in-Chief was less fulsome than he had hoped but an introduction to the Venetian governor was obtained and suitable lodgings were arranged.

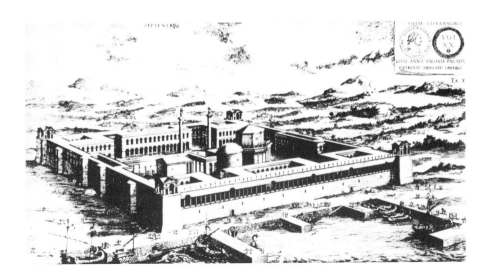

Plate 23   Diocletian's Palace, Split. From J.B. Fischer von Erlach, *Entwurf in der Historischen Architektur* (1721).

93

He was soon pleased to discover how much he could improve on the earlier accounts: 'how little justice former descriptions and unskillful drawings had done to it'. He soon discovered also that the task was far from easy: 'first from the numbers of modern houses built within the walls of the palace and even upon its own foundation; secondly from the inhabitants having pulled to pieces and utterly destroyed some parts of the antique work; and lastly from their having so blended the ancient and modern work together by repairs and alterations that it was not without great difficulty they could be distinguished.' He overcame these but his digging in the foundations caused some officers to suspect that he was not planning the ancient remains but surveying the fortifications. Reports were made to the Governor and it became known that the promised permit had not arrived from Venice. General Graeme interceded on Adam's behalf but suspicions were revived and his activities were watched. Digging was prohibited and no drawing of fortifications was permitted. By the 28th August he could leave Spalato, which he had enjoyed: 'The people are vastly polite, everything vastly cheap, a most wholesome air and glorious situation.' He spent five weeks at Spalato, during which four people were constantly at work.

The magnificent folio was published in 1764. With its 61 plates printed by F. Bartolozzi and A. Zucchi at Venice, Adam aspired to emulate the work of Piranesi.[228] Though the work bore his name and the text was his, the volume is the product of others' work, notably of Clérisseau. As a memoir of architecture the volume is magnificent. The drawings remained the fullest and most reliable portrayal of the remains for more than one and a half centuries. In the matter of detail they have been found to be inexact. One cannot be certain if some features were really there or whether they have been merely restored as a consequence of imagination and wish to demonstrate 'l'ésprit de système' as Hébrard put it.[229] The drawings are constructed with a symmetry between left and right that is not always faithful to the original (Figure 13).

The five weeks spent in Spalato had an immediate impact on Adam's work. At Rome he had spent years studying remains of public buildings but in Dalmatia he saw surviving remains of a private residence. The influence of what he saw was apparent directly and indirectly in much of his later work. Perhaps the most striking testimony of this is the building erected by Adam and his three brothers alongside the Thames in London. As a private venture they leased a site that sloped steeply down from the Strand to the river in order to erect a great terrace of fine houses upon huge vaults, some in double tiers, fronting the river. Though it drove them nearly to bankruptcy, the brothers' venture — named Adelphi from them — dominated the river below Westminster. It brought the south façade of Split to the heart of London and its destruction must be accounted one of the great losses in the past architecture of the capital.[230]

Later in the eighteenth century, though before Napoleon had extinguished the Republic of Venice in 1797 (Plate 24), the French artist and engraver L.F. Cassas made numerous drawings of the remains. These were published by Joseph Levallée in 1802, together with a memoir of Cassas' journey through Istria and Dalmatia made in 1782.[231] The collection includes a drawing of the peristyle by Clérisseau. The accompanying text adds little to the general account of Adam and others, but the drawings, in contrast, appear a more faithful record of the surviving remains, not only of the palace but also of the medieval city. In this respect their value exceeds the works by Adam and his draughtsmen, and the high estimate of the quality of Cassas' work which already prevailed in the nineteenth century has proved more than justified .

A century of Austrian rule brought at first neglect, then an extensive programme of restoration on the mausoleum and belfry, directed at first by the architect Alfred Hauser.[232] Early in the century there were two major studies of the remains, by the Austrian Georg Niemann at public expense (1905–09) and by the French architect Ernst Hébrard and historian Jacques Zeiller (1906–10) with private funds (Figure 13). Both have their merits and together remain the basis on which modern research, inevitably more fragmented, can be based.[233] All those who have ever studied the fascinating remains at Split would agree that there is yet a great deal to be learned about this unique residence erected for a retired Roman emperor nearly seventeen centuries ago.

Reflection upon the remains at Split inevitably turns back to their creator. In the year when Adam's great folio was published the greatest of modern historians, contemplating the ruins of Rome, conceived his great history. Gibbon's perceptive judgement on Diocletian the emperor holds much that is true also of his *villa*:

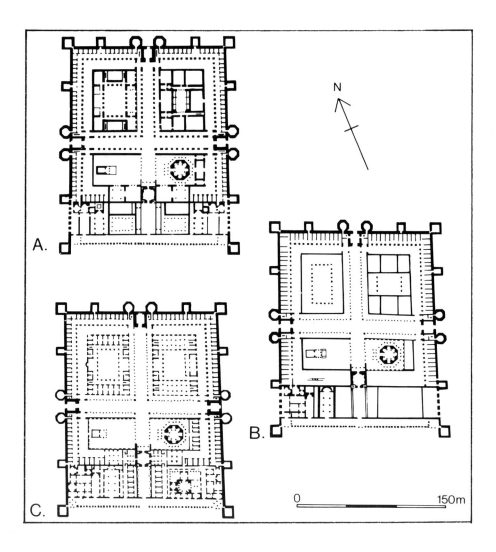

Figure 13   Restored plans of Diocletian's Palace by Adam (1764), Nieman (1910) and
Hébard-Zeiller (1912).

'The valour of Diocletian was never found inadequate to his duty, or to the occasion; but he appears not to have possessed the daring and generous spirit of a hero, who courts danger and fame, disdains artifice, and boldly challenges the allegiance of his equals. His abilities were useful rather than splendid — a vigorous mind improved by the experience and study of mankind; dexterity and application in business; a judicious mixture of liberality and economy, of mildness and vigour; profound dissimulation under the disguise of military frankness; steadiness to pursue his ends; flexibility to vary his means; and, above all, the great art of submitting his own passions, as well as those of others, to the interest of his ambition, and of colouring his ambition with the most specious pretences of justice and public utility. Like Augustus, Diocletian may be considered as the founder of a new empire. Like the adopted son of Caesar, he was distinguished as a statesman rather than as a warrior; nor did either of those princes employ force, whenever their purpose could be effected by policy.'[234]

Plate 24   Medal of Napoleon struck to mark annexation of Dalmatia by Treaty of Pressburg (Bratislava) in 1806. On reverse the mausoleum is portrayed as 'Temple de Jupiter à Spalato'. *Photo: Courtesy of the Trustees of the British Museum.*

REFERENCES

1   At long last there is now available a more than adequate account of Diocletian's reign in Stephen Williams, *Diocletian*, reviewed and, with some reservations, welcomed. by T.D. Barnes, *LS*, 5 July 1985. *New Empire* by that scholar is an invaluable guide to 'the basic factual framework for a period in the history of the Roman Empire which is both obviously significant and notoriously obscure' (Preface p. vii). Another welcome addition to the bibliography of this period is J. L. Creed's edition and translation of Lactantius' *De Mort. Pers.*

2   See the catalogue established by T.D. Barnes, 'Imperial Campaigns, AD 285–311', *Phoenix* 30 (1976), 174–93.

3   Though he survived the nineteenth anniversary of his accession on 7 March 180, he died on the 17th of the same month.

4   See Barnes, *New Empire* 30 f. His birthday is furnished by papyri, *P. Beatty Panop* (ed. T.C. Skeat, Dublin, 1964), 2, 164, 173, 181/2, 193/4, 262. The *Epitome de Caesaribus* 39, 7, compiled nearly a century later, states that he lived sixty-eight years. Since it implies that he died early in 313, it would place his birth, depending on base date and method of computation, on 22 December 243, 244 or 245. As regards his origin it seems certain that he came from Dalmatia and probably from Salona. Eurtropius ix 19, 2 and *Epitome de Caesaribus* 31, 1 specify Dalmatia, Aurelius Victor, *De Caesaribus* 39, 26 Illyricum. Lactantius *De Mort. Pers.* 19, 6, when describing his journey into retirement, 'in patriam dimittitur', may be specific to Salona, rather than just Dalmatia. Nothing can be inferred from the name C. Valerius Diocles. The gentilicium is very widespread. The cognomen Diocles, a common freedman's name, is attested on an epitaph at Salona, *CIL* III 4809 (Aurelius Diocles). A story that his mother's and his birthplace were named Dioclea, *Epitome de Caesaribus* 39, 1, has since given rise to much speculation and local legend that he was born at Doclea, a city in the extreme south of Dalmatia. The story of Eutropius ix 19 and *Epit. de Caels.* 39, 1, is that he was of most humble origins *(obscurissime natus),* that many recorded that he was son of a clerk *(scriba)*, others that he was freedman of a senator named Anullinus. C. Annius Anullinus, consul 295 and proconsul of Africa 306–7 *(PLRE* 1, 79), may be of the same family, perhaps the son of Diocletian's patron.

5   He may have enjoyed the distinction of a consulship (suffect) in this year. The Paschal Chronicle (Mommsen, *Chronica Minora* 1, p. 229) enters Diocletian and Bassus between the *ordinarii* of 283 and 284. But the correct date may be 284 – from accession on the 20th November. See Barnes, *New Empire* 93.

6   For the origins of Diocletian and his colleagues see Barnes, *New Empire* 30 ff. For the earlier Illyrian emperors see the entries in *PLRE* vol. 1.

7   *PLRE* 1, 574 f. and Barnes, *New Empire* 37 f. His birthplace and place of burial was Romulianum, allegedly derived from his mother Romula, now to be identified with

Gamzigrad in the Black (Crni) Timok valley west of Zaječar, more than twenty miles from the Danube (see p. 78). On Dacia Ripensis as a 'dynamic region', see R. Syme, *Historia Augusta Papers* (Oxford, 1983), 64 f.

8   R. Syme, *op. cit.* (note 7) 63 ff. Constantine was born on 27 February 272 or 273; Barnes, *New Empire* 39 f. Then Naissus was still in Moesia Superior, becoming part of Dardania probably under Diocletian; see A. Mócsy, *Pannonia and Upper Moesia* (London, 1974), 274.

9   Marcus Aurelius Valerius Maximianus was born *c*. 250 near Sirmium, *Epit. de Caes.* 40, 10. For the dates of his elevation see Barnes, *New Empire* 4.

10   Williams, *Diocletian* 56–60. The *Panegyric* xi (iii) of Mamertinus describes the celebration. Its imagery and rhetorical presentation is examined by Sabine MacCormack, *Art and Ceremony in Late Antiquity* (Berkely, 1981), 22 ff., a work that has much to offer students of the Later Roman Empire.

11   Williams, *Diocletian* 63 ff.

12   See Stephen Johnson, *Late Roman Fortification* (London, 1983), and J. Lander, *Roman Stone Fortification* Brit. Arch. Rep. Int. 206 (Oxford, 1984), esp. 181–93, on Diocletianic activity.

13   That is clearly to be understood from the Birdoswald inscription, R.G. Collingwood and R.P Wright, *The Roman Inscriptions of Britain* (Oxford, 1965), vol. 1, no. 1912, which records that under the Tetrarchy there were 'restored the commandant's house, which had been covered with earth and had fallen into ruin, and the headquarters building and the bath house'.

14   Two places named Iovia and another Iovalia on the strategic road along the Drava valley (Mursa-Poetovio) appear on the *Peutinger Map* (see below note 55). On the frontier are the forts Ad Herculem (Pilismarót), and a 'contra Herculia'- across the river between Brigetio and Aquincum, and in the area of Sirmium. On the Sopianae-Brigetio road there is Iovia and Herculia, and Ad Herculem on the road from Naissus to Lissus on the Adriatic.

15   Limestone plaque 1.84 by 0.91 by 0.28m: 'Impp. Caess. C. Val. Aur. Diocletianus et M. Aur. Val. Maximianus pp. ff. invicti Augg. et Fl. Val. Constantius et Galerius Val. Maximianus nobilissimi Caesares Germanici Maximi Sarmatici Maximi pro futurum in aeternum reipublicae praesidium constituerunt'. The name of Maximianus was erased after his *damnatio memoriae* in 311. Published by Aleksandrina Cermanović Kuzmanović, *Starinar* 28–9 (1977–78), 1979, 127–34 and plate IV, 2 = *AE* 1979, 519. The scale of rebuilding under the Tetrarchy has been revealed by the recent rescue excavations in the Danube gorge; see *Starinar* 33–4 (1982–83). From the lower Danube three, possibly four, building inscriptions proclaimed the new defences in similar fashion: 'after the hordes of the enemy were subdued and peace for their world secure (the emperors) established this military, strongpoint to last for ever', 'post debellatas hostium gentis confirmata orbi suo tranquillitate in aeternum constituere praesidiu(m) *ILS* 641 (Sexaginta Prista); *AE* 1966, 357 (Transmarisca); *AE* 1936, 10 (Durostorum). The fourth is a fragment from Seimeni Mici in the

Dobrudja, *CIL* III 7487 = Popescu, *Inscripţiile* 205.

16 See Williams, *Diocletian* chs. 7–11 (p. 91–150).

17 The *Edict on Maximum Prices* mentioned also by literary sources, e.g. Lactantius *De Mort. Pers.* 7, 6–7 (quoted below p. 5), known from many copies exhibited in provincial cities, mainly in the East, is perhaps the best known of his reforms. The standard edition is S. Lauffer, *Diokletians Preisedikt* (Berlin, 1971) supplemented by E.J. Doyle, *Hesperia* 45 (1976), 77–97. A parallel text and translation (though inevitably out-of-date) by Elsa Rose Graster was included in the fifth volume of Tenney Frank's *Economic Survey of Ancient Rome* (Baltimore, 1940), 307 ff. Discovery, at Aphrodisias in Asia Minor, of a copy of a hitherto unknown Currency Reform issued in the same year reveals that there was much more to Diocletian's economic policy than the seemingly naive prices edict: see Kenan T. Erim, Joyce Reynolds and Michael Crawford, *JRS* 61 (1971), 171–7.

18 Lactantius, *De Mort. Pers.* 7, 2–10 (translated by J.L. Creed).

19 Lactantius, *De Mort Pers.* 8, 2.

20 Williams, *Diocletian* 111–14.

21 For example the striking portrait of Gallienus, taken as symbolic of Hellenic revival, in the Museo Nazionale delle Terme at Rome, on which see now Anna Marguerite McCann, 'Third-Century Portraiture', *ANRW* II, 12, 2 (1981) 632–7 and plate IX.

22 There is a large and increasing literature on Roman imperial portraiture and its changing styles. Recent comprehensive works include M. Bergmann, *Studien zum römischen Portrat des 3. Jahrhunderts n. Chr*, Antiquitas 18 (Bonn, 1977), 138 ff. The recently acquired basalt head in Worcester Art Museum, Worcester, Mass., Williams, *Diocletian* plate 2 (opposite p. 112), has been generally accepted as Diocletian, as first proposed by R. Teitz a decade ago, cf. A.M. McCann, *op. cit.*; (note 21), 637–40 and pls. XII–XIII. The identification is accepted by C.C. Vermeule, 'Tetrarchs True and False', *Art of Antiquity, Iconographic Studies Department of Classical Art*, Boston Museum of Fine Arts, (Boston, 1980), 59–76. For the most recent discussion of Diocletian's portraits see H.P. L'Orange, *Das spätantike Herrscherbild von Diocletian bis zu den Konstantin - Söhnen 284/361 n. Chr* (Das römische Herrscherbild III.4), Berlin, 1984, 13–24, with catalogue pp. 95–103 (including the Worcester head, p. 103).

23 McCann *op. cit.* (note 21) p. 639. That author cites the two pairs of figures attached to columns now in the Vatican Library. For all the notions of inborn divinity it is hard not to agree with the comment of Donald Strong, *Roman Art* (London, 1976), 151: 'quaint, dwarf-like creatures in military dress, each with one arm flung around its companion and a globe in the other hand. There is no majesty here ...'. Though powerful authority stands in support, it seems hard to credit that the well-known marble head from Nicomedia, with beard and wreath, portrays Diocletian; see McCann, *op. cit.* (note 21), 639 f. One may note the comment of Fittschen in K. Fittschen and P. Zanker, *Katalog der römischen Porträts in den Captolinischer Museen und den anderen kommunalen Sammlungen in der Stadt Rom* Bd. I (Mainz,

1985), 143, note 4: 'There is still lacking a truly authenticated portrait of Diocletian, to cite only the worst gap for portrait art from the beginning of late antiquity. The likeness from Nikomedia remains, if it does indeed depict Diocletian, iconographically so far completely isolated'.

24   *De Mort. Pers.* 15: So now the emperor began to rage not only against the members of his houshold but against everyone, and first of all he compelled his daughter Valeria and his wife Prisca to be polluted by doing sacrific'. The text is furnished by Lactantius, *De Mort. Pers.* 34. For an account of the Great Persecution see W.H.C. Frend, *Martyrdom and Persecution in the Early Church* (Oxford, 1965), 477–521. *Acts of the Christian Martyrs* ed. H. Musurillo (Oxford, 1972) includes texts and translations of the *Acta* of several Diocletianic martyrs.

25   Diocletian's tirade, in an edict addressed to Julianus the proconsul of Africa, suggests a fanatical hatred not evident in his measures against Christians: 'We order that founders and their leaders, along with their abominable writers, should suffer a more severe penalty, to be burnt in the flames'(in *Mosaicarum et Romanarum legum collectio,* in Riccobono, *Fontes Iuris Romani Antejustiniani* (Florence, 1940), vol. 2, 550 f.). See Williams, *Diocletian* 83 f. The date is evidently 302 rather than 297: see Barnes, *New Empire* 55, note 41.

26   Lactantius, *De Mort. Pers.* 11, 1: 'deorum montium cultrix, mulier admodum superstitiosa'. Perhaps it was the cult of Silvanus, Diana and Liber Pater, attested in Moesia and Dacia, as suggested by J. Moreau in his commentary on Lactantius *(Sources chrétiennes* 39, Paris 1954).

27   Lactantius, *De Mort. Pers.* 10 preserves the story how Diocletian flew into a rage when informed that some of his own attendants *(ministri)* were Christian and had, through their presence, frustrated the reading of entrails by the *haruspices*. 'He ordered that not only those who were attending the rites but all who were in the palace should do sacrifice, and that any who declined should be punished by whipping; he also sent letters to commanders ordering that soldiers too should be compelled to perform the abominable sacrifices, and that any who disobeyed should be discharged from military service. This far his rage and anger went; he did nothing further against the law and religion of God'. The date of the incident is either 299 or 300.

28   Lactantius, *De Mort. Pers* 11, 7–8. In his *Life of Constantine* 2, 50, Eusebius records that, as reported by Constantine, the oracle replied: 'the righteous on earth were an obstacle to his telling the truth'. Diocletian's regard for Didyma is reflected in two dedications found at the shrine, erected under the proconsul T. Flavius Festus (in 286–93, *PLRE,* 1 335), which dedicated statues of Zeus and Leto: A. Rehm, 'Kaiser Diokletian und das Heiligtum von Didyma', *Philologus* 93 (1938), 74–84, and *Didyma* II: *Die Inschriften* (1958), nos. 89–90.

29   The triumphal arch on the Via Lata was dismantled under Pope Innocent VIII in 1491. Its remains were later removed to the Medici Villa on the Pinciana. The reliefs were incorporated in the villa's garden façade. In 1785 the pedestals were removed to the Boboli Gardens in Florence. Its ornament included: a relief VOTIS X ET XX with the

personification of a conquered province; the Dioscuri; Victory; a captured Dacian and a captured German. See E. Nash, *Pictorial Dictionary of Ancient Rome,* vol. 1 (London, 1961), 120 ff. A relief above the left side-passage on the north side of the Arch of Constantine shows behind the rostra a monument of five standing columns, and remains from the site confirm that these were erected on ornate bases for the *vicennalia* of the Augusti and *decennalia* of the Caesars, celebrated on the 20th November 303. One base with carved relief has a cartouche inscribed CAESARVM DECENNALIA FELICITER. Another (now lost) was inscribed AVGVSTORVM VICENNALIA FELICITER, and another, perhaps the base of the Jupiter Column, VICENNALIA IMPERATORVM. Excavation on the site revealed the foundations of the bases and a plinth of curved steps *(hemicyclum).* See Nash, *op. cit.* (above), 198 ff., and for a full account of remains and a reconstruction, H. Kähler, *Das Fünfsäulendenkmal für die Tetrarchen auf dem Forum Romanum (*Monumenta Artis Romanae III) (Cologne, 1964).

30   Lactantius *De Mort. Pers.* 7. An edict issued from Nicomedia on 28th August 304 attests the presence of Diocletian, *Cod Just.* III 28, 26. Lactantius asserts that illness affected his mental balance, and the same story is found in Eusebius, *Hist. Eccl.* 13, 11.

31   Lactantius, *De Mort. Pers.* 19, 5–6. 'Huic (Maximin Daia) purpuram iniecit suam qua se exuit, et Diocles iterum factus est. Tum descenditur, et reda per civitatem veteranus rex foras exportatur in patriamque dimittitur'. Thus Lactantius, *De Mort. Pers.* 26, 6.

32   Eutropius, ix 27, locates the estate in Lucania, cf. Orosius vii 28, 5, Zosimus ii, 10.2 and Zonaras xii, 32. A Panegyric alludes to the *otium suburbanum* of Maximiamus, vii (vi) 11.3.

33   Eutropius ix 28: 'Diocletianus privatus in villa, quae haud procul a Salonis est, praeclaro otio senuit, inusitata virtute usus, ut solus omnium post conditum Romanum imperium ex tanto fastigio sponte ad privatae vitae statum civilitatemque remearet; contigit igitur ei quod nulli post natos homines, ut cum privatus obisset, inter divos tamen referretur'

34   Aur. Victor, *Liber de Caes.* 39, 48: 'Et quamquam aliis alia aestimantibus veri gratia corrupta sit, nobis tamen excellenti natura videtur ad communem vitam spreto ambitu descendisse'. For literary and epigraphic references to Diocletian as senior Augustus after retirement see. W. Ensslin, *RE* VIIA, 2491.

35   Lactantius, *De Mort. Pers.* 10, 1: 'scrutator rerum futurarum; Aur. Victor, *Liber De Caes.* 39, 48: 'imminentium scrutator'. Cf. Zosimus, ii, 10, 5.

36   Williams, *Diocletian* 194–200, offers a summary account of events down to the deaths of Maximianus and Galerius.

37   Diocletian, for the only time after abdication, held the consulship (his tenth) in 308. Lactantius, *De Mort. Pers.* 29, 1–2, states that Diocles was sent for by Galerius to sanction the appointment of Licinius, whereas it was Maximian's intention to eliminate Galerius. The meeting is placed at Carnuntum, legionary fortress, major

town and provincial capital on the Danube east of modern Vienna, by Zosimus ii, 10, 4, who describes it as a 'Celtic town'. Lactantius implies that Licinius was invested on the spot with status of Augustus in the presence of the others 'itaque fit utroque praesenti'. Licinius's investiture is dated to 11th November by a Chronicle: *Consularia Constantinopolitana* (Chron Min. *p.* 231): 'levatus Licinius Carnunto III id. Nov'. The dedication of a statue erected late in the reign of Licinius (AD 322–23) at Salsovia (Mahmudia) in the northern Dobrudja appears to give the 18th November as the date of accession, *ILS* 8940 = Popescu, *Inscripţiile* no. 271b (with photo). W. Seston, *Römische Forschungen in Niederösterreich III* (Graz, 1956), 175–86, separates the Conference in 207, from the formal investiture of Licinius on 18th November 308. Diocletian, Maximian, Galerius and Licinius are the *Jovii* and *Herculii* who dedicated to Mithras at Carnuntum: 'D(eo) S(oli) i(nvicto) M(ithrae) fautori imperii sui Jovii et Herculii religiosissimi Augusti et Caesares sacrarium restituerunt: *CIL* III 4413 = *ILS* 659.

38 *Epit. de Caes.* 39, 5–6: Diocletianus vero apud Nicomediam sponte imperiales fasces relinquens in propriis agris consenuit. Qui dum ab Herculio atque Galerio ad recipiendum imperium rogaretur, tamquam pestem aliquam detestans in hunc modum respondit: 'Utinam Salonae possetis visere olera nostris manibus instituta, profecto numquam istud temptandum iudicaretis'. *(H)olera* denotes any variety of green vegetables but is generally rendered as cabbages.

39 Lactantius, *De Mort Pers.* 35; 39 and 41.

40 Lactantius, *De Mort. Pers.* 51: 'Valeria too, after wandering through various provinces over fifteen months in the dress of a woman of the people, was finally recognisd at Thessalonica; she was arrested and punished along with her mother. The women were led to execution while many watched with pity for so mighty a fall; their heads were cut off and their bodies thrown into the sea. Thus their virtue and their rank were their undoing'. Throughout Lactantius' refrences to these ladies reflect his belief that they were Christians who held to their faith (see note 24 above).

41 Lactantius links his death with the *damnatio memoriae* of Maximian ordered by Constantine and implies 311 or 312. In the view of Barnes, *JRS* 63 (1973), 32 ff., cf. *New Empire* 31 f., this testimony is to be preferred to that which links the death with the marriage of Licinius and Constantia in February 313 *(Epit de Caes* 39, 7; Socrates, *HE 1* 2, 10) or the 315 or 316 of Jerome's *Chronicle,* 230 Helm, whence derive Prosper Tiro *(Chron. Min.,* I p. 448) and a later Gallic Chronicle *(Chron. Min.,* I p. 643); Zosimus 2, 8, 1; *Paschal Chronicle,* p. 523 Dindorf; or 316 in *Consularia Constantinopolitana (Chron. Min.,* I p. 231) and a papyrus fragment of a Greek chronicle, *P. Berol* 13296. Barnes suggests that if the date of 316 arises from a confusion of the latter's consuls *Sabino et Rufino* with those of 311 *Volusiano ets' Rufino* then the preferred date must be 3rd December 311.

42 For a general account, see Wilkes, *Dalmatia* 46 ff.

43 Wilkes, *Dalmatia* 220 ff.

44 At last five major roads constructed by the legionary garrison were completed in AD

17 and 20. Wilkes, *Dalmatia* 452–5. The title of governor changed to *praeses* in the later third century: see p. 98 and n. 187.

45 John Bradford, *Ancient Landscapes* (London, 1957), 183 ff.

46 Ronald Syme, *Colonial Elites* (Oxford, 1958), 5: 'one can distinguish in the first century of the Roman Empire three rich, populous, and dynamic regions'.

47 For an account of their careers see Anthony R. Birley, *The Fasti of Roman Britain* (Oxford, 1981), 106 ff. and 118 ff.

48 Anthony Birley, *Septimius Severus* (London, 1971), 35 ff.

49 For an analysis of the Salona population se G. Alföldy, *Bevölkerung und Gesellschaft der römischen Provinz Dalmatien* (Budapest, 1965), 108–118.

50 For an enthusiastic description of these qualities see Williams, *Diocletian* 26 f.

51 The road from Salona via Klis to the Andetrium (Muć), a native stronghold and later a Roman military base, was named *via Gabiniana* after Aulus Gabinius, Caesar's ill-fated commander in the civil wars: see Wilkes, *Dalmatia* 41 f. The name appears on the monument commemorating its construction by the seventh legion in AD 17 (*CIL* III 3198 a = 10156 and 3200): 'item viam Gabinianam ab Salonis Andetrium aperuit et munit per leg(ionem) VII'.

52 Jackson, *Dalmatia* 2, 105 ff. His three volumes remain one of the best introductions to the history and monuments of Dalmatia.

53 For the likely remains of the shrine see J. and T. Marasović, *VAHD* 61 (1959), 1963, 122–33.

54 See Wilkes, *Dalmatia,* for a general account of the Greeks in the area. On the decree recording the settlement at Lumbarda, W. Dittenberger, *Syll. Inscr. Graec.* 141 see D. Rendić-Miočević, *VAMZ* 4 (1970), 31–44. Tragurion and Epetion are named as possessions of Issa in 158 BC, Polybius xxxii 9. Some archaeologists have asserted a Greek or rather Hellenistic origin for Salona. The evidence remains inconclusive. See the judicious summary by Christoph W. Clairmont, *Excavations at Salona, Yugoslavia 1969–72* (New Jersey, 1975), 1–7.

55 Now available in facsimile with commentary by Ekkehard Weber, *Tabula Peutingeriana Codex Vindobonensis 324* (Vienna, 1976). On the current state of knowledge see A.L.F Rivet and Colin Smith, *The Place-Names of Roman Britain* (London, 1979), 149 f.

56 *Not. Dign. Occ.* xi 48: 'procurator gynaecii Iovensis, Dalmatiae – Aspalato'. On its date and purpose see J.C. Mann, in R. Goodburn and P. Bartholomew (eds.), *Aspects of the Notitia Dignitatum* (Brit. Arch. Rep. Int. 15, Oxford, 1976), 1–9.

57 Ed. Pinder and Parthey (Berlin, 1860), 209, 8 and 380, 9. On this work in general see Rivet and Smith, *op. cit.* (note 55) 185 ff.

58 Const. Porphyr., *DAI* c. 29, 8, 23; 30, 14, 15, 30, and commentary, p. 107. Thomas,

Arch. c. 4: 'hoc scilicet edificium spelatum dictum est a pallantheo, quod antiqui spatiosum dicebant palatium'. On this author see Jackson, *Dalmatia* 2, 75 f. Note also Jerome's *Chronicle of Eusebius* (p. 230 Helm): 'Diocletianus haut procul a Salonis in villa sua Spalato moritur et solus omnium inter deos privatus refertur' (on the reading see below, note 150); and Prosper Tiro, *Epit. Chron. (Chron. Min.* I, p. 448): 'Diocletianus haut procul a Salonis in villa sua Spalato moritur'.

59   Pliny, *Nat. Hist.* xii, 110, cf. Liddell and Scott, *Greek-English Lexicon;* Wagler, *RE* 2 (1896), 1710 f. In modern times the *convulvulus tenuissimus* (Croatian slamečak), which flowers in May, has grown on the Marijan peninsula: Bulić-Karaman, 14 f.

60   Bulić-Karaman, 17; cf. *Split Excavations* I, 13 ff. Most likely the foundations seen by Bulić belong to the medieval building upon the Roman mosaics. A fine cornice-moulding, dated to the first or second century, is held to indicate an earlier building on the site (Marasović, *Diocletian Palace* Supplement pl. 14 with photograph); but this may have reused material brought from elsewhere for the construction of the residence.

61   Hébrard-Zeiller, 20.

62   See J.B. Ward-Perkins, 'Quarrying in Antiquity: Technology, Tradition and Social Change' *(Mortimer Wheeler Archaeological Lecture 1971)* London, 1972 (= *Proceedings of the British Academy* 77 (1971), 137–58).

63   The best general account remains F. Bulić, 'Materiale e provenienza della pietra, delle colonne, nonchè delle sfingi del Palazzo di Diocleziano a Spalato e delle colonne ecc. delle basiliche cristiane a Salona', *Bull. Dalm.* 31 (1908), 86–127. On the Brač quarries, see p. 86 ff. For some valuable observations on the technique of stone construction at Split, see Michael R. Werner, 'The Development of Stonework in Roman Dalmatia: Continuity and Innovation', in *Classics and the Classical Tradition* ed. E. Borza and R. Carruba, Pennsylvania State University Press 1973, 178–87.

64   On condemnation to mines or quarries see now Fergus Millar, *PBSR* 52 (1984), 137 ff.

65   Dedications to him by soldiers are known from the Brohl valley near Andernach in Germany *(CIL* XIII 769s ff.). It appears to have been predominantly a military cult; see L. Cesano, *Dizonario Epigrafico* (ed. E. D. Ruggiero) vol. 3, p. 718. A dedication to Hercules by *lapidarii* of the Fourth and Seventh legions was recently discovered on the rock face of the Danube gorge in Upper Moesia near the famous road of Trajan, M. Gabricevic, *Arheološki Vestnik* (Ljubljana) 23 (1972), 408 ff. (= *AE* 1973, 473).

66   *CIL* III 10107 (= *ILS* 3458): 'Herculi Aug(usto) sac(rum) Val(erius) Valerianus mil(es) cum insisterem ad capitella columnarum ad t(h)ermas Licinian(a)s qua(e) [f]iun[t] Sirmi' (the last three words in the reading of Mommsen *CIL* ad loc.). Sirmium, for long an imperial residence, was also the scene of a major building programme under Diocletian, reflected in the *Acta* of the IV *Coronati* martyrs during the Great Persecution: 'the emperor Diocletian ordered that columns and capitals should be cut by masons from the porphyry quarries. M. Mirković, in *Sirmium* (ed. V.

Popović) vol. 1, Belgrade 1971, 37. The location of these quarries, presumably producing a local version of red granite, must lie somewhere in the Sirmium area; see A. Mócsy, *Pannonia and Upper Moesia* (London, 1974), 326. Mommsen notes, *CIL* ad loc., that near this inscription lay uninscribed tombstones and altars, and some unfinished portraits, indicating the range of products produced in that quarry.

67   For a descripfion of Šibenik Cathedral and an account of the role of George (Orsini) the Dalmatian, see Jackson, *Dalmatia* 1 378 ff.

68   Bulić, *op. cit.* (note 63).

69   In modem times it was still obtained by the inhabitants of Solin for use in their houses, R. Egger, W. Gerber, et al., *Forschungen in Salona* I (Vienna, 1917), 57 ff.

70   The most likely source for the clay is the Dujmovača valley between Split and Solin, Bulić-Karaman (Serbocroatian ed.), 22, n. 45.

71   See Appendix XV of Wilkes, *Dalmatia* 499–502, and *id.* in A.McWhirr, (ed.), *Roman Brick and Tile*, Brit. Arch. Rep. Int. (Oxford, 1979), 65–72. The principal factories were the *Pansiana*, *Q. Clodius Ambrosius* and *L. Titius Hermeros*. The *Solonas* or *Solonate* bricks were not, as formerly believed (Bulić-Karaman, 20), from a local Salona factory, but from Aemilia in Italy Their distribution in Dalmatia is almost entirely confined to Salona, though they are missing from Split.

72   See J.B. Ward-Perkins, 'Dalmatia and the Marble Trade', *Disputationes Salonitanae* (Split, 1970), 38–44.

73   Tripolitania, more especially Lepcis Magna, is a case in point: 'The marble architecture of second-century Tripolitania is as truly imperial in character as the sandstone and limestone architecture of the first century is provincial': John Ward-Perkins, *JRS* 41 (1951), 95.

74   On the quarries see Nuşin Asgari, *Proceedings of the Xth Congress of Classical Archaeology 1973* (Ankara, 1978), 467–80. See J.B. Ward-Perkins, 'Nicomedia and the Marble Trade', *PBSR* 48 (1980), 40 ff.

75   The identifications of marbles and granites were made by Bulić, *op. cit.* (note 63). Nothing remains of the embellishments reported in earlier accounts of the North Gate. Adam shows three small free-standing columns still in position and they were still there in 1820. Venetians or local citizens may have removed them; see Bulić-Karaman, 26, (with n. 15 on p. 50 f. of Serbocroatian edition). For an account of surviving columns of imported marbles see above p. 20.

76   Heinz Kähler, 'Split and Piazza Armerina-Residences of Two Emperor-Tetrarchs', *Urbs* 4 (1961–62), 1965, 201 f. and figs. 6–9 and 159 (English summary); *Die Villa des Maxentius bei Piazza Armerina,* Monumenta Arts Romanae XII, (Berlin, 1973), 21: 'Daruber hinaus aber die betreffenden Kapitelle in Piazza Armerina, Spalato und Saloniki, wenn auch nicht von der gleichen Hand, so doch in der gleichen Werkstatt und zur gleichen Zeit entstanden'. In the view of P. Pensabene (see below note 181) no such comparison is possible since the capitals in the Sicilian villa include some re-used pieces of the first and second centuries.

77   Fragments of white marble veneer 20mm thick were noted in the *piscina* of the East Baths, and a deposit of veneer fragments, evidently reused, was found in a small chamber adjoining the East Baths *palaestra: Split Excavations* 1, p. 29 and 26 with plate 15a.

78   Bulić-Karaman, 46, citing a sixteenth-century local account (see below p. 50), and plate 62 for illustration of fragments (now lost) of glass mosaic discovered on the dome of the vestibule during restoration *c.* 1900. See also Hébrard-Zeiller, III, noting that *tesserae* were of red and green glass and white limestone, though no pattern was discernible.

79   Before the recent excavations (1968–74) several floor mosaics had been recorded:

(a) Three floor mosaics, panels or 'carpets' in and around a court east of Vestibule Basement were described by Niemann, 108 fig. 141, and Hébrard-Zeiller 141, n. 2, and Bulić-Karaman, pl. 68. They were re-excavated during restoration work in 1957–58; Marasović, *Urbs* 34, with illustrations. Those on the north have been covered again, those on the south have been incorporated as a floor of the Town Planning Institute.

(b) A mosaic with a pattern of circles and diamonds was discovered by Niemann, fig. 112 f., after trial excavation in front of St Philip's Church in Grga Ninski Poljana in the south-east of the north-east quarter. It was later exposed: Bulić-Karaman, pl. 67.

(c) A mosaic east of the vestibule, recorded but not illustrated by Niemann, 109.

A summary catalogue of ten mosaics (including loose fragments) discovered during excavations in 1968–74 is furnished by Claudia Smith, *Split Excavation* 3, 142 f. with illustrations. Four corridor mosaics (two of which had been revealed in the 1925 excavation, see Bulić-Karaman, pl. 69) around the courtyard *(?palaestra)* north of the East Baths:

(d) north corridor: pattern of octagons and crosses; pl. 1, A–C.

(e) east corridor: eight-point lozenge stars defining large squares; pl. III A and B.

(f) south corridor: knucklebones in oblique rows; pl. II C.

(g) west corridor: adjacent lozenges and squares; pl. II A–B.

(h) (i) and (j) fragments of three mosaics from debris in the same area, patterns unrecognizable.

(k) fragments of mosaics from East Baths, with blue glass, green and colourless *tesserae*.

(l) two fragments, limestone and glass *tesserae* from area south-west of 'Triclinium' in east range of private apartments.

(m) West Baths. Three fragments, limestone and glass *tesserae* with thin sheet of gold-coloured material adhering to clear glass *tesserae*.

The known mosaics of Galerius' Palace at Thessalonica are also simple geometric compositions, albeit of superior quality to those at Split. See *Arch. Deltion* 19 3 (1964), pl. 376.

80   Described by Jequier: Les monuments égyptiens de Spalato', in Hébrard-Zeiller, 209 ff., cf. Bulić-Karaman, 46–9 and pl. 34–7.

81   It is possible that the head of a sphinx, somewhat damaged, found in 1908 during excavations at Salona, came originally from Diocletian's residence: F. Bulić *Bull. Dalm.* 31 (1908), 101, with pl. XIX, 1–2 and Bulić-Karaman, 49, with pl. 37. A mutilated sphinx was found during excavation east of the Vestibule: Marasović, *Urbs* 31.

82   The four statue-bases are illustrated in scale drawings in Kähler, *op. cit.* (note 76, second item, above). An example of the problems in the interpretation of surviving portraits is furnished by a recent discussion of two heads: Nenad Cambi, 'Two heads of Tetrarchic period from Diocletian's Palace at Split', *Arch. Iug.* 17 (1976), 1979, 23–8 with figs. 1–3. Two life-size heads in limestone are re-used in a house balcony (Ispod uve no. 3). The older head has been identified with Maximianus Augustus, the younger with a god – possibly one of the Dioscuri.

83   A striking figured tombstone of the Tetrarchic era was discovered re-used as a grave-cover in the Christian cemetery at Marusinac, near Salona: D. Rendić-Miočević, *VAHD* 56–59/2 (1954–57), 156–62 with pl. XIV = Šašel, *ILIug* 1940–60 *(Situla 5* Ljubljana 1963), 60, no. 126. It was erected by Aurelius Leontius, *vir ducenarius* and *decurio* of Salona, and also *curator* (financial commissioner) of the colony, to his son Aurelius Valeri(a)nus, private secretary of two emperors in the secretariat department who died in the city of Nicomedia *(exceptor imp(eratorum duorum) in officio memori(a)e qui aput civitatem Nicomediensium fati munus complevit)* . It is tempting to imagine some link with his fellow Dalmatian Diocletian through service in his capital Nicomedia.

84   As regards the duration of building work, it is worth noting the judgement of T. Marasović, cited by Williams, *Diocletian* 256, n. 1: 'the palace must have been begun in the 290s at the latest, if it was to have been even near-complete in 305'. It will have been imprudent, to say the least, for any architect or engineer to make enquiry as to when the emperor expected to reside there.

85   ZOTIKOS occurs in Latin 105 times at Rome, *CIL* index s.v. and H. Solin, *Die Griechischen Personennamen in Rom: Ein Namenbuch (CIL* Auctariorum), Berlin-New York 1982, 2, 827 f. From Salona: *CIL* III 9003 (Clodia); 13926 (Coylius), 2626 (frg.); and at Srinjine in Poljica, 14650/1 (Julius). Another name PHILŌT on the base of a column in the Mausoleum portico, J. and T Marasović, *Diocletian Palace* Supplement pl. 16, is also a well-attested freedman or slave name, Philota(s); Solin, *op. cit.*, 880 f. Conceivably, it was already on the column before it reached Dalmatia.

86   Many mason's marks were revealed on the inner wall-faces of the South-east tower during recent excavations *(Split Excavations* 1, 22 and drawings 7–10), also on the inside face of the perimeter wall a little to the north of the tower *(Split Excavations* 2, drawing 6). It is worth noting that the impression of eastern craftsmen at Split is corroborated by several elements in the construction and ornament of the residence.

These include use of dressed stone, the façade of the Porta Aurea and the brick vaulting in the dome. For some acute reflections on the mixture of East and West at Split, see J.B. Ward-Perkins, *Roman Imperial Architecture,* 2nd ed. London 1982, 458.

87 Nor is it certain that it was a Christian symbol: for its popularity in pagan times see J.M.C. Toynbee, *Animals in Roman Life and Art* (London 1973), 206–8.

88 Though the drawings in Robert Adam's volume record some detail which has since disappeared, our knowledge of the remains is based on works published during this century. The full surveys of Niemann and Hébrard-Zeiller remain the basis for any description. Their findings are summarised and supplemented by Bulić-Karaman. After the Second World War investigations during restoration by the Town of Split from 1945 to 1952, mainly in the northern and eastern areas, were published by C. Fisković, with drawings by J. Marasović. A new programme of excavation and restoration, mainly in the southern area, began in 1955 and its important findings published in *Urbs* 1961–62 (1965), 23 ff. The most important finds are illustrated in Marasović, *Diocletian Palace* Supplement (Enclosure) at the end of the volume. Results of joint excavations by the University of Minnesota and the Town Planning Institute, Split, undertaken in 1968–74 are currently being publishd in *Split Excavations.* For a survey of the principal discoveries see S. McNally, 'Ausgrabungen im Diokletianspalast zu Split', *Antike Welt* 10 (1979) Hft. 2, 35–46.

89 'The ground-plan quadrangle, 215 meters long and 180 metres wide (total area of some 30,000 meters), was slightly deformed owing to its being adapted to the configuration of the ground, i.e. by its northeastern corner being moved a little to the west, in order to avoid the natural ridges in that area.' Marasović, *Diocletian Palace* Supplement fig. 34. Nonetheless it might be more realistic to assume that the irregularity in plan was the result of simple error.

90 Niemann, 10 ff.; Hébrard-Zeiller, 29 ff.; Bulić-Karaman, 22–4; Marasović, *Diocletian Palace* 12–14.

91 In 1971 the basement and upper level of the gallery were examined and a section of the façade recorded. See *Split Excavations* 2, 39–41 and drawing 16. The height of the façade above the cornice level remains uncertain, though J. Marasović supports the view that seven courses of rusticated masonry are part of the original façade.

92 *Split Excavations* 2, 43 and drawing 16. No trace of the central loggia remains. That on the west was fairly well-preserved until comprehensive restoration in 1906. The two columns of the east Loggia, which survived until the beginning of the ninth century, were damaged by incorporation in a new building, although the raised architrave is well-preserved.

93 *Split Excavations* 2, 41, with drawing 13, where remains of three are recorded.

94 *Split Excavations* 1, 21–4 and drawings 7–10. The door in the west wall of the South-east tower could have led to dry land or a small jetty. Today the foundations of the South Wall lie at least 2m below sea level. Older records from the eleventh century record that the sea reached the wall in the ninth century and an inscription of 1626

records that in the seventeenth century water still reached the south façade.

95 Niemann, 21 ff.; Hébrard-Zeiller, 39 ff.; Bulić-Karaman, 24–8; Marasović, *Diocletian Palace* 13 f. The nomenclature of the gates follows Bulić-Karaman, 24. In Marasović, *Diocletian Palace* 12–14, the South Gate is called *porta Aenea* and the East Gate *porta Argentea*.

96 The true load-bearing function of the gate arches, not as would appear from outside merely decorative relieving arches surmounting the horizontal lintel, is emphasisd by A.J. Brothers, *Greece and Rome* 19 (1972), 184 f.

97 They are unusual portraits: 'these little faces with their ears and horns would seem to be far more in place in a medieval cathedral than over a Roman gateway', Brothers. *op. cit.* (note 96), 184.

98 If Niemann's suggestion that an older arrangement of the bases, with the largest at the central line of the façade, is correct, then there will have originally been five bases, possibly adding Jupiter to the Tetrarchs as was the case with the monument in the Roman Forum near the *rostra*. See H. Kahler, *op. cit.* (note 29), 6 f. and *Urbs* 4, 1961–62 (1965), 101 fig. 5, for a reconstruction of five bases *in situ*. The evidence for their having been bases is not strong. Older views of the gate (Niemann, 24) suggest that the largest base (0.82m high) was once located on the central axis of the gate. Since the two smallest bases are almost identical in height (0.62m and 0.61m) then the missing fifth base would have matched the fourth surviving base (0.75m). No trace of a fifth base has ever been reported.

99 S. Matijvić, *Urbs* 4, 1961–62 (1965), 18.

100 Niemann, 86 ff.; Hébrard-Zeiller, 53 ff.; Bulić-Karaman, 31 f.; Marasović, *Diocletian Palace* 14 f.

101 Split Excavations 2, 62 ff. and drawing 25

102 *Split Excavations* 1. p. 13 f. and drawing 13.

103 Niemann, 86 ff.; Hébrard-Zeiller, 56 ff.; Bulić-Karaman, 31 f.; Marasović, *Diocletian Palace* 15 and Supplement figs. 26–9.

104 On the association of this porch with its central raised arch to Roman images of victory, see below n. 169.

105 Bulić-Karaman, p. 33, n. 36.

106 Described by B. Gabričević, *VAHD* 63–64 (1961–62), 1969, 113 ff.

107 Suggested by F. Weilbach, *Strena Buliciana* (Zagreb/Split, 1924), 123 f., stressing the military analogies of the interior plan.

108 Bulić-Karaman, plate 67.

109 Marasović, *Diocletian Palace* 15.

110 Niemann, 44 ff.; Hébrard-Zeiller, 63 ff.; Bulić-Karaman, 33–6; Marasović, *Diocletian Palace* 15 ff.

111   The suggestion that the Peristyle may have had a wooden roof, by J. Strzygowski, *Markstein* 330, may be discounted; see Bulić-Karaman, 34. The rectangular sockets and cement on the top of the architraves were identified by Hébrard-Zeiller, 65, as likely fixings for statues. Their existence is doubted by Bulić-Karaman since they could not be located during restoration work in 1906.

112   The pediment of the porch had long shown signs of instability. Before Adam's time a wall (now partly removed) was inserted to support the pedimental arch. In 1911, when it was discovered that the two central columns had splayed 17cms out of true, the weakness was countered by insertion of the bronze clamps still in position.

113   Summarised in *Urbs* 4, 1961–62 (1965), 30 f., cf. Marasović, *Diocletian Palace Supplement*, fig. 32.

114   This arrangement is described by E. Dyggve, *Urbs* 4, 1961–62 (1965), 55–60. See also note 161 below.

115   Niemann, 62 ff.; Hébrard-Zeiller, 69–99; Bulić-Karaman, 36–43; Marasović, *Diocletian Palace* 17 f. In recent years there has been excavation in the south-west angle of the precinct: *Split Excavations* 2, 47–52 and drawings 17–21.

116   Split Excavations 2, 51 f. and drawings 17 and 21.

117   Niemann's reconstruction, 71, fig. 90 and plate XII, reproduces the arched pediment of the Peristyle. Hébrard-Zeiller, 82 f., suggests a horizontal lintel with simple attic below the level of the window. A third reconstrucuon, of a simple low pediment with ridged roof corresponding to that of the peripteron, was proposed by G. Stratitimović, *Bull. Dalm.* 34 (1911), 99–107, cf. *Jahreshefte des Österreichischen Archölogischen Instituts* 19 (1913), Beiblatt 169 ff. It was based on the traces of the original porch noted during restoration in the nineteenth century and was favoured by F. Weilbach, *Strena Buliciana* (1924), 119–23.

118   The east wall was demolished for the Sacristy and Choir of the Cathedral constructed in 1602; see Bulić-Karaman, 148. It was the work of Marc' Antonio de Dominis, Archbishop of Split 1602–16, whose colourful career included a spell in England as Dean of Windsor under James I. See Jackson, *Dalmatia* 2, 9–14.

119   For identification of the stones in the Mausoleum, F. Bulić, *Bull. Dalm.* 31 (1908), revised by J.B. Ward-Perkins, *op. cit.* (note 72), 39 and 44. Both upper and lower columns were removed during restoration in 1880–85 and, along with many other architectural fragments of the original fabric, were taken to the Archaeological Museum. They have been replaced by replicas in modern materials.

120   At this point the dome is 1.50m thick. Some have doubted whether the pine cone is an original embellishment. If it is not, it is hard to imagine who would have taken the trouble to place there such a heavy object.

121   The deified Augustus was presumably placed in a porphyry sarcophagus, perhaps on a dais in the centre. In conversation at Split (1970) H. Kähler suggested that fragments of imperial red porphyry now in Split Museum may derive from it. The incident of AD 356, Amm. Marc. xvi 8, 4 (see below p. 83), reveals that the Mausoleum was still

intact at that date. Possibly the tombs of his wife Prisca and daughter Valeria were placed in the semi-circular niches. This was the arrangement at Ravenna a century later, where Galla Placidia was flanked by Honorius and Valentinian III.

122 Counting anticlockwise from the north side of the porch, two columns (nos. 14 and 15) on the east side were removed during construction of the Cathedral choir in 1602, while a third (no. 7) is missing on the south. They were taken to the Benedictine church at Sustjepan (St Stephanus de pinis) and then, after its destruction, to the cemetery chapel, on the small headland at the west end of the Bay of Split. The stones of the ambulatory columns have been identified as follows (by Bulić, *Bull. Dalm.* 31 (1908), p. 94, revised by J.B. Ward-Perkins, *op. cit.* (note 72), 44): Grey Egyptian granite (*mons Claudianus*), nos. 4 and 1; Red Egyptian granite (Assuan), nos. 5–6 and 22–4; *Breccia Corallina* (?Aegean), nos. 8, 19 and 21; *Proconnesian*, nos 13 and perhaps 12, 17 and 18. Nos. 9–11 are of inferior quality grey granite, not Egyptian.

123 Fully illustrated in Marasović, *Diocletian Palace*, plates 57, 59, 61–89. The hunting scenes gave rise to a local belief that the building was a temple of Diana the huntress.

124 M. Vickers *PECS* 912 f., with bibliography. In the event Galerius was buried at Romuliana, now identified with Gamzigrad (see below, p. 77) On the Mausoleum of Maxentius see now J.J. Rasch, *Das Maxentius Mausoleum an der via Appia in Rom* (Mainz, 1984).

125 Niemann, 80 ff.; Hébrard-Zeiller, 100 ff.; Bulić-Karaman, 57–61; Marasović, *Diocletian Palace* 18–21 and Supplement fig. 33.

126 A smaller column in local stone with a fragment of architrave above the capital, built into the side of an adjoining house, do not derive from the Temple. See Bulić-Karaman, 58.

127 Marasović, *Urbs* 31–3; also *Diocletian Palace*, Supplement fig. 36. These circular structures within the *temenos* are unusual and may be another example of 'eastern' elements at Split.

128 Niemann, 55 ff.; Hébrard-Zeiller, 110 ff.; Bulić-Karaman, 62 f.; Marasović, *Diocletian Palace* 21

129 Fragments found during restoration are illustrated in Bulić-Karaman, plate 62.

130 Room 11B on the numbering scheme for the basements; Marasović, *Urbs* 1 26 f.

131 *Split Excavations* 2, 5 3–8, plates 26–7 and drawings 22–4. The basic outline of the building is partly preserved in the baroque building above it, formerly the house of the Tartaglia family, now the Hotel Slavija.

132 *Split Excavations* 1, 27–33, with plates 16–25 and drawings 11–13.

133 Three of these blocks were found during excavation re-used in the wall of a later house, *Split Excavations* 1, plate 24b. A fourth, discovered during sewer excavations in the nineteenth century, was removed to the ambulatory on the north side of the Mausoleum. It was recorded by Niemann, 109 and fig. 43. The provenance of other architectural fragments, including a fine *anta* capital (*Split Excavations* 1, plate 17b),

remains uncertain.

134   *Split Excavations* 1, 13–16, plates 4–6 and drawing 3. Another part of the baths complex may be a small chamber (*c.* 3.60m square) on the south-east within the line of the perimeter piers, and with entrances on the east and west. It was filled with a variety of building debris including fragments of marble veneer laid as a floor; *Split Excavations* 1, 26 f., plates 14–15 and drawing 3. A sounding between the apse and the *palaestra* court revealed a pedestalled column base, evidently still in situ: *Split Excavations* 2, 59 f. and plate 28B.

135   The mosaics were reported by Niemann, p. 108, fig. 141, and Hébrard-Zeiller, p. 141, n. 2, and Bulić-Karaman, plate 68 (see above note 79). They were fully exposed during excavations and restoration in 1955; see Marasović, *Urbs* 30 and fig. on p. 34; *Diocletian Palace* 20 and Supplement, fig. 38. No trace has since been located of the mosaic on the west side of the vestibule reported by Niemann, p. 109, n. 3. It may have belonged to another court, perhaps connected with the West Baths.

136   Niemann, 95 ff.. and 104 ff.; Hébrard-Zeiller, 115 ff.; Bulić-Karaman, 61–6; Marasović, *Urbs* 24 ff. T. Marasović, 'Gli appartamenti dell' Imperatore Diocleziano nel suo palazzo a Split', *Acta Ad Archaeologiam et Artium Historiam Pertinentia* (Inst. Rom. Norvegiae) 4 (1969), 33–40; *Diocletian Palace* 20–3.

137   Limited clearance of debris and refuse which had for centuries filled the basements was undertaken before the First World War. Much of the work was organised by Niemann, at public expense in 1905–09, and Hébrard, from private funds in 1906–10. Systematic clearance began on behalf of the Split authorities by J. and T. Marasović in 1955–65, and the results summarised in *Urbs* 23–54. Most of the basements have now been cleared. Recent excavations have succeeded in elucidating something of the arrangements at the east end where the vaults have collapsed: *Split Excavations* 2, 13–38. The numbering of rooms follows that of Marasović.

138   For a close-up view of the ornament, see Marasović, *Diocletian Palace*, plate 29.

139   Two wells of Roman date, square and stone-lined, were found in the basement of the gallery 10m west of the South Gate. In the opinion of the excavators they were sunk before construction of the basements. East of the South Gate, at a distance of between 5 and 15m, several fragments of a cornice moulding dated to the first or early second century were found. See Marasović, *Urbs* 24 and 30; *Diocletian Palace*, Supplement fig. 15. The walls of the upper gallery were clad with white marble and alabaster, and the floor paved with white marble.

140   The misalignment of the principal north-south axis of Peristyle and Vestibule, a few degrees to the west, is largely absorbed by the tapering width of the light-wells from 0.5m to 2.00m. It is suggested that the light-wells and corridors in the east of the range are less constricted than those in the west because the raised arch in the east half of the south façade, is located farrher from the centre than that on the west.

141   See the view of restored remains at the upper level, Marasović, *Diocletian Palace*, Supplement fig. 43. In 1970 a shaft 1m square outside the south-west angle was cleared to the depth of 7.8m at which point sea-water entered. It may have been a

References

drainage shaft rather than a latrine. It was filled with debris, including a fourth-century coin, pottery, amphorae and lamp fragments and many worked fragments of marble, inlcuding Phrygian, Proconnesian, Numidian, Pentelic, Euboean Cipollino, African red and a local onyx. See *Split Excavations* I, 37 and plates 26a–c. The octagonal triclinium at Split, as revealed by recent investigations, has much in common with the great octagon at Thessalonica, though the latter (diagonal 29.50m) is on a larger scale than Split (diagonal *c*. 13m). The notion that the octagon at Thessalonica was the imperial dining-room appears to have been advanced first by H. Torp, 'Den Keiserlige Dionysos: Galerius' Festal i palasset i Thessaloniki', *Kunst og Kultur* 57 (1974)153–64 (cited by O. Nicholson, *Byzantion* 54 (1984) 258 n. 22). I owe this suggestion and references to Dr. R.J.A. Wilson.

142 Between the Triclinium complex and the east perimeter wall recent excavations have revealed five or six rooms occupying the rectangle of *c*. 30 by 15m, with a few remains of the corresponding chambers at the upper floor level. See *Split Excavations* 2, 15–38, plates 4–11 and drawings 4–12.

143 Before recent clearance and restoration it was entered by an opening from the narrow street to the north. Within the walls at basement level on either side of the apse one spiral stairway led to the street and the other to the upper floor. Arches supported bridges across the light-wells at the upper level to allow direct access to the smaller hall (4A) and the corridor (8) through narrow passages in the thickness of the side walls. They may also have served to transfer lateral thrust of adjacent structures onto its 3m thick walls.

144 A row of triangular recesses held horizontal beams at the level where the vaults spring from the top of the wall. The cross-timbers were supported by vertical timbers set in the floor, some remains of which were found still in position. See the illustration in Marasović, *Urbs* 30.

145 Bulić-Karaman, 67 (more fully in Serbo-croatian ed. 109–14).

146 The aqueduct entered the city near the north-east gate (*porta Andetria*) of the *urbs nova*. See *Forschungen in Salona*, ed. Gerber, Egger, etc. vol. I (1917), 140 and Wilkes, *Dalmatia* 361, fig. 16.

147 The surviving remains were restored in 1878–79. See the views of its condition before and after in Bulić-Karaman, plates 71–2. The work was commemorated by a grandiloquent inscription worthy of the Tetrarchs: 'Auspiciis Francisci Josephi I imperatoris Austriae regis Dalmatiae Antonius Bajamonti praefectus Spalatinus aquae ductum ab imperatore Diocletiano magnifice extructum longa vetustate dilapsum sumptibus de aerario publico et arca municipali suppeditatis restauravit aquamque saluberrimam in urbem deduxit anno sal. MDCCCLXXIX'

148 The drainage system from north to south and east to west within the walls has not yet been fully traced. A main sewer ran beneath the Peristyle with side channels from the Mausoleum and Temple precincts (see above p. 46) Some drains were found during recent excavations in the south-west corner of the Mausoleum precinct, *Split Excavations* 2, 48 ff. Near the East Gate a vaulted sewer 0.6–1.1m wide was discovered intact, Marasović, *Diocletian Palace,* Supplement, fig. 45. A drain cover

with the pattern of a six-leaf rosette was found in situ near the surviving corner pillar at the intersection of the main streets, Marasović, *Diocletian Palace,* Supplement, fig. 28.

149   Several local traditions relate to the aqueduct. One from Venetian times explains that water was required for the breeding of trout of which Diocletian was especially fond. The modern reservoir alongside the old road to Solin bore a medallion portrait of Diocletian, the sole commemoration in Split of its founder and most famous resident.

150   'in villa quae haud procul a Salonis est', Eutropius ix 28; 'haut procul a Salonis in villa sua Spalato', Jerome *Chronicle*, p. 230 Helm; on the reading of the text see J. Zeiller, *Mélanges Cagnat* (Paris, 1912), 421 f. where this is preferred to 'in villae suae palatio'; 'Diocletianus haud procul a Salonis in villa sua Spalato moritur', Prosper Tiro, *Epit. Chron.* (Chronica Minora vol. 1, p. 448).

151   Libanius *Or.* XI, 203–7 and also Theodoret, *Hist. Eccl.* 4, 23. On the Palace see G. Downey, *A History of Antioch in Syria* (Princeton, 1961), 318–23.

152   See Donald Strong, *Roman Art* (Harmondsworth, 1976), plate 250. The similar composition on the Lampadius diptych at Brescia is illustrated by E. Dyggve, *Urbs* 4 (1961–62), 57, fig. 3.

153   The first exposition that Split was a version of the Roman palace is J. Strzygowski, *Markstein.* Cf. also E. Dyggve, *Ravennatum Palatium Sacrum. La basilica ipetrale per ceriimonie. Studi sull' architettura dei palazzi della tarda antichita* (Copenhagen, 1941), and H.P L'Orange, *Art Forms and Civic Life in the Late Roman Empire* (Princeton, 1965), 70–6. Note the criticism by A.M. Schneider, *Antiquity* 24 (1950) 139, n. 34, of the notion that the Peristyle was a form of 'open-air basilica'.

154   Duval, *Urbs* 67–95. This section owes much to the exposition of Duval which contains a full consideration of 'palatial' and 'ceremonial' theories of Strzygowski, Dyggve and others.

155   On Philippopolis see H.C. Butler, *American Archaeological Expedition to Syria 1899–1900, II (Architecture)*, New York 1904, 382–4 with fig. 135. See also subsequent literature cited by J.-P Rey-Coquais, *PECS* 705f. On the Palace at Thessalonica see the plan of the remains included with *Tabula Imperii Romani* K 34 (Ljubljana, 1976) and the bibliography in M. Vickers, *PECS* 913. G. Knithakes, 'To octagono tes Thessalonikes', *Arch. Deltion* 30, 1 (1975), 90–119; and N.C. Moutsopoulos, 'Contribution a l'étude du plan de ville de Thessalonique à l'époque romaine', *Atti del XVI. Congresso di Storia dell' Architettura, 1969* (Rome, 1977), 187–265.

156   Duval, *Urbs* 74: 'En définitive, si on doit choisir un term précis Split serait plutôt un 'château'. Ce mot évoque en français (et non le Latin *castellum*) à la fois la résidence d'apparat et ses nécessaires dépendances, une architecture monumentale, et souvent une enceinte fortifiée'.

157   Perge in southern Turkey is a good example; see George Bean, *Turkey's Southern Shore* (London, 1968). 54. For a plan of the Great Palace at Constantinople see S.

Miranda, *Autour du Grand Palais des Empereurs Byzantins* (Mexico, 1968), and, in simplified form, in Averil Cameron, *Corippus* (see below note 159), 22.

158   See Noel Duval, 'Que savons-nous du palais de Théodoric à Ravenne?', *MEFR* 72 (1960), 337–71; and 'Comment reconnatre un palais impériale ou royale? Ravenna et Piazza Armerina', *Felix Ravenna* 115 (1978), 27–62.

159   The basic studies are by A. Alföldi, 'Die Ausgestaltung des monarchischen Zeremoniells und römische Kaiserhofe', *Rom. Mitt.* 49 (1934), 1–118; 'Insignien und Tracht der römischen Kaiser', *Röm. Mitt* 50 (1935), 1–171, reprinted as *Die Monarchischen Repräsentation im römischen Kaiserreiche* (Darmstadt, 1970). For court ceremonial in sixth-century Constantinople see Averil Cameron, *Fl. Cresconius Corippus: In laudem Iustini Augusti minoris: libri IV* (London, 1976).

160   The point is made clear by the photograph in Duval, *Urbs* 80, fig. 3. The theory of the 'open space' was advanced in studies (cited by Duval) by L. Crema, 'Osservazioni sull' architettura tardoromana', *Studi in onore di A. Calderini e R. Paribeni* (Milan, 1956) 3, 585–6; 'Il palazzo di Diocleziani a Spalato', *Corsi di cultura sull' arte ravennate e bizantina* (Ravenna, 1960) 2, p. 44–51 and *Architettura Romana* (Turin, 1959) 614–15. See the comments of Duval, *Urbs* 79.

161   See the paper by E. Dyggve, *Urbs* 4, 1961–62 (1965), 55–60 (published posthumously in Serbo-Croat with English summary), and the discussion of this and other theories relating to Vestibule and 'tablinum' by Duval, *Urbs* 87 ff.

162   For a general study see Stephen Johnson, *Late Roman Fortifications* (London, 1983), though its scope is confined mainly to North-west Europe. See also J. Lander, *Roman Stone Fortifications*, Brit. Arch. Rep. Int. 206 (Oxford, 1984). In the matter of Split the author (on p. 50) observes: 'the use of polygonal towers in both the fort at Burg-bei-Stein and in Diocletian's own Palace in Split suggests that the emperor had some hand in making the choice for the towers on the Rhine fort'. The inference is hardly valid since the towers at Burg-bei-Stein are placed astride the wall, their interiors are D-shaped and only the front is polygonal. Polygonal towers are reviewed by Lander, *op. cit.*, 244–6, noting that they are not a common feature of late antiquity. He cites single gates at Aquincum and Oudenburg, also Chancy in Raetia. None matches Split precisely, for which the closest parallel is Romuliana (Gamzigrad; see below p 77). For the plan of the gate at Salona see Wilkes, *Dalmatia* fig. 21 and on Augustan gates in general see Johnson, *op. cit.* fig. 4. The late fortifications in Pannonia (Fenekpuszta, Környe, Kisárpás, Ságvar and Alsóheténypuszta) are described by Johnson, *op. cit.* p. 123 with fig. 45; cf. Lander, *op. cit.* p. 235.

163   Der Diokletianspalast von Split im Rahmen der spätrömischen Militärarchitektur', *Antike Welt* 1979, Heft 2, 47–55 The approach is in places rather overschematic and the suggested typologies may prove less clear-cut when more is known of late forts' interior arrangements. Nevertheless, this section is indebted to Fellmann's choice of examples for analogy and his interpretation.

164   Both Deir el-Kahf and Qasr Bshir have yielded inscriptions of AD 306. See Lander, *op. cit.*, p. 185. See D. Tudor, *Oltenia Roman*, (3rd ed. Bucharest, 1968), 449 ff. with

plan and restoration; also the booklet *Drobeta* (Bucharest, 1965), 36. For a different dating of the phases, see Radu Florescu, *Studien zu den Militärgrenzen Roms, Vorträge des 6. internationalen Limeskongresses in Suddeutschland* (Beihefte der Bonn. Jahrb. Bd. 19, (Cologne-Graz, 1967), 144–51.

165   See Iain Browning, *Palmyra* (London, 1979), 184 ff. and fig. 125 (plan).

166   See Fellmann, *op. cit.* (note 163), 50, citing R.E. Brunnow and A.V Domaszewski, *Die Provinz Arabia* vol. 2 (Strasbourg, 1905), 8–13 and plate 41.

167   On Dionysias, modern Qasr Qarun north of the Fayum, in general see S. Shenouda, *PECS* 276 f. and on the Diocletianic fort see J.-M. Carrié, *MEFRA* 86 (1974), 819–50. The latter's hypotheses are discussed, with some criticisms, by J. Lander, *op. cit.* p. 190.

168   On Hadrian's Wall see J.J. Wilkes, 'Early fourth-century lrebuilding in Hadrian's Wall Forts', in Jarrett, M.G., and Dobson, B. (eds.), *Britain and Rome* (Kendal, 1966), 114–38, and C. Daniels in *Roman Frontier Studies* 1979, eds. W.S. Hanson and L.J.F Keppie, Brit. Arch. Rep. Int 71 (Oxford, 1980), 173–93. R. Florescu, *op. cit* (note 164), 148, fig. 4.

169   On the Sword of Tiberius (now in the British Museum) see G. Lippold, 'Zum Schwert des Tiberius' *Festchrift Rom.-Germ. Zentralmuseums* Mainz, 1952, 1, 4 ff. See also Susan Walker and Andrew Burnett, *Augustus*. British Museum Occasional Paper No. 16, 1981), 49–55. For the façades of the *principia* see Rudolf Fellmann, *Der Principia von Vindonissa und das Zentralgebäude der römischen Lager und Kastelle* (Brugg, 1958), fig. 32 and 65. Against the 'military' interpretation it can, as R.J.A. Wilson has observed, be argued that the *leitmotif is* surely that of civilian military architecture which by the Late Empire had become inextricably mixed up with the divinity of the Emperor's personage and with court ceremonial, and concluded that 'the porch is like a temple-front, where entrance is gained to the divinity that dwells within'. (*pers. comm.*)

170   See N. Duval, *Urbs*, 78 ff.

171   N. Duval, *Urbs*, 87 ff.

172   N. Duval, *Urbs*, 90 ff.

173   N. Duval, *Urbs*, 92 ff. The great basilica of the villa at Piazza Armerina may be compared with that at Split (see below p. 77). Their similar dimensions (*c*. 30m by 14m) see R.J.A. Wilson, *Piazza Armenina* (London, 1983), 109–10 n. 65. In the matter of scale comparisons with such halls in palaces of ruling emperors (Maxentius' (via Appia), 38m by 19m; Trier, 67m by 27m; Thessalonica, 53m by 25m) emphasise that the provision at Split was modest, testimony to the reported intention of the former Augustus to live as a private citizen. A similar difference of scale is evident from comparing the Split triclinium (n.141 above) with the octagon at Thessalonica.

174   See Edith Mary Wightman, *Roman Trier and the Treviri* (London, 1970), 145 f. and, for a reconstruction (by Sheila Gibson) of the façade, J.B. Ward-Perkins, *Roman Imperial Architecture* (2nd. ed. Harmondswonh, 1981), 244. The use of light-wells

for the ground floor chambers at Nennig also invites a comparison with Split. Another parallel is furnished by the late-fourth century residence at Konz, on an eminence at the confluence of the Saar and Mosel. Its façade has a portico with projecting wings, with a large central chamber behind. See Edith Mary Wightman, *op. cit.*, 166–7 and, more recently, *Triers Kaiserresidenz und Bischof-sitz* (Rheinisches Landesmuseum, Trier), Mainz, 1984, 310–4. The representations of villas on African mosaics has been exhaustively treated by T. Sarnowski, *Les représentations de villas sur les mosaïques africaines tardives* (Wroclaw, 1978). Apart from African examples, some villas in Pannonia appear, at a more modest level, to aspire to a similar image though none is known to have had an arcaded frontage. See E.B. Thomas, *Römische Villen in Pannonien* (Budapest, 1964). In a different medium a fourth-century *situla* in Rome portrays the façades of four villas, all with corner towers and (at ground level) arcading between. See A. Carandini, *Bull. Comm. Arch. Comunale di Roma* 79 (1963–64), 147–63 (including a discussion of villas and mosaics and a list of parallels).

175   Now described and analysed by Katharine M.D. Dunbabin, *The Mosaics of Roman North Africa* (Oxford, 1978), 120 ff., 252 no. 32 and plate XLIII, no. 109. The mosaic comes from a luxurious residence in Carthage. The name of the owner is deduced from the scene in the lower register where a man presents the lord with a scroll bearing the letters IV(LIO) DOM(INO).

176   The same type of villa is depicted on mosaics in the three apses of an elegant house at Thabraca (Tabarka) on the coast west of Carthage. They are also dated to the late fourth century and were evidently by the same workshop which produced the Julius Dominus mosaic. In the right apse the residence has a less elaborate façade but is still a substantial building. That in the left is a simple working form, surrounded by a jumble of outbuildings and sheds. The central apse has a fine residence on the scale of that on the Carthage mosaic. Together they may be intended as the three traditional parts of a rural establishment, the *villa urbana*, *villa rustica* and *villa fructuaria* of Columella, *De Re Rustica* i 6, 1, as suggested by Dunbabin, *op. cit.* (note 175), 122 f.; 271 and plates XLIV, XLV, nos. 111–13

177   Argued by I. Bojanovski, 'Mogorjelo: Rimsko Turres', *Glasnik Zemalskog Muzeja u Sarajevu* N.S. 24 (1969), 137–63.

178   Ejnar Dyggve and Hermann Vetters, *Mogorjelo: Ein spätantiker Herrensitz in Dalmatien* (Schriften der Balkankommision, Antiqu. Abt. Hft. XIII), Vienna-Graz-Cologne, 1966.

179   The reconstruction is criticized by Duval: 'l'élevation de la façade resulte, à Mljet comme à Mogorjelo, d'une pure imagination graphique', *Bull. Soc. Nat. Antiqu. de France* 1971, p. 108, citing the summary of a paper in *Bulletin du comité international d'histoire de l'art* 4 (1969), 13. The remains of what appear an ancient or early medieval building on a bay in the north of the island Mljet (ancient Melite) have attracted some interest since the Second World War. The site is today named Polača and the principal remains comprise two polygonal towers at the water's edge linked by a corridor which fronts a large hall (12m by 26m) with an apse at the rear, and to which smaller chambers were attached on either side (see Wilkes, *Dalmatia*,

pl. 50). It is constructed in a local stone which splits easily into long strips, suitable for making thin masonry courses. Dyggve identified and restored it as a late Roman palatial residence, *Palladio* 9 (1959), 19–26; later M. Cagiano de Azevedo suggested that it was the residence of a minister of Odovacar who received its revenues on 18th March 489, according to a document in the Ravenna archive, 'Il palatium di Porto Palazzo a Meleda', *Atti del Convegno int. sul tema tardo antico e alto medioevo* 1967 (Accademia dei Lincei, Rome 1969), 273–83. Both the identification as a late Roman palace and the historical connection with Pierius the minister of Odovacar are pure conjecture and appear too easily to have been transformed into ascertained fact. See Duval, *op. cit.* (this note) 105–9.

180   For a brief description see J.B. Ward-Perkins, *op. cit.* (note 174) 460–4. For a full account of the villa, see now R.J.A. Wilson, *Piazza Armerina* (London, 1983), which offers a skilful dissection of the arguments for imperial ownership, on p. 86–92.

181   See note 76 above. Against this R. Pensabene has observed that the capitals at *Piazza Armerina* include re-used items and range in date from the second century to the early fourth, *MEFRA* 83 (1971), 207–19.

182   See A. Carandini and others, *Filosofiana. The Villa of Piazza Armerina* (Palermo, 1982), 54 ff.

183   The discovery was reported in the Belgrade newspaper *Politika* during July 1984, for news of which I am grateful to M.R. Werner of New York State University, Albany. An account of earlier discoveries is furnished by M. Čanak-Medić, *Kasnoantička Palata Arkhitektura i Prostorni Sklop, Saopshtena XI Republičkog Zavoda za Zaštitu Spomenika Kulture SR Srbije*, Belgrade (with French summary), supplemented by D. Srejović, A. Lalović and Dj. Janković, 'Gamzigrad', *Starinar* 31(1980), 65–80 (with French summary,) For illustrations of some of the mosaics see D. Srejović, 'An Imperial Palace in Serbia', *Illustrated London News* (Archaeology 2909), October 1975, 97–9. There is now the well illustrated exhibition catalogue by D. Srejović, D. Janković, A. Lalović and V Jović, *Gamzigrad Kasnoantički Carski Dvorac* (Belgrade, 1983). This includes the discovery of a second palace in the north-east angle of the fortified area. (I am grateful to R.J.A. Wilson for news of this publication and its contents.) For a more accessible account of the site see M. Mirkovic and V. Popović, in D. Papenfuss and V.M. Strocka (eds.), *Palast ünd Hütte* (Mainz, 1982), 486–92.

184   It is observed by R.J.A. Wilson, *Piazza Armerina*, 84, that this arrangement of a residence within a larger perimeter is similar to Fenékpuszta (perhaps the ancient Valcum) at the south end of Lake Balaton in Hungary. It lay not far from the main Sirmium to Trier road and occupied a rectangle 392 by 348m with forty-four corner, interval and gate towers. Alongside was a late Roman cemetery Its purpose has been debated. The internal arrangements do not suggest a strictly military function: a storehouse, Christian basilica and a large residence *c.* 100 x 50m. Nothing of the luxury or decoration of Gamzigrad has been found. Perhaps it was the centre of a large imperial estate; see A. Mócsy, *Pannonia and Upper Moesia* (London, 1974), 303 f. It will be of great value if more could be excavated of the great imperial residence at Mediana (Brzi brod), 4km east of Naissus (Niš) in Moesia Superior (for

a plan of the remains see D. Srejović *et al.* (1983), cited in note 183, p. 64, fig. 55). Built by Constantine (who may have been born there) it was used by several emperors during the fourth century. Some state rooms, with mosaic floors, marble veneer and stucco moulding have so far been uncovered; Mócsy, *op. cit.* p. 302 and plate 43b; also James Wiseman in *PECS* 605 f. (Naissus).

185 She came from the north of the Danube and fled to Dacia (Nova) from the Carpi, Lactantius *De Mort. Pers.* 9, 2. A devout pagan she worshipped 'the mountain gods' (deorum montium cultrix); see above note 26. The origin of the place-name is given by the *Epitome de Caesaribus* 40, 16: '(Galerius) ortus Dacia Ripensi ibique sepultus est; quem locum Romulianum ex vocabulo Romulae matris appellarat'.

186 An ambition to enjoy a carefree and calm old age is attributed to Galerius by Lactantius, *De Mort Pers.* 20, even as early as the time of Diocletian's abdication.

187 The known late third- and fourth-century governors of Dalmatia are listed in *PLRE* 1, 1091 f. For a general account of Dalmatia in the late empire see Wilkes, *Dalmatia* 416 ff.

188 The state textile factory at Bassiana in Pannonia appears to have been removed to Salona around this time: *Not. Dign. Occ.* xi, 46. On refugees in Dalmatia at this period see J.J. Wilkes, *Phoenix* 26 (1972), 377–93.

189 See Wilkes, *Dalmatia* 423–7. The administration was in the charge of a *comes*. One of these, Osvin, is named by Cassiodorus, *Variae* ix 9 (cf. *RE* 18 (1942), 1854) and another may be recorded on a bilingual epiraph at the Salona, a *comes* Eufrasius (*CIL* III 9534 = 117 cf. *PLRE* 2, 425).

190 Amm. Marc. xvi 8, 4. In the fifth century the intact state of the Mausoleum is suggested by an allusion in a poem of the fifth-century Sidonius Apollinaris, *Carm.* xxiii 495: 'hinc at balnea non Neroniana nec quae Agrippa dedit vel ille, cuius bustum Dalmaticae vident Salonae, ad thermas tamen ire sed liberat privato bene praebitas pudori'.

191 Exiles at Boa include Florentius *magister officiorum* in 361 *(PLRE* 1, 363), Hymetius, former proconsul of Africa, in 371–72 *(PLRE* 1, 447) and the heretic Jovinianus *(Cod. Theod.* xvi 5, 53) on 6th March 412. The first two both returned to public life after a brief sojourn. There is no obvious reason, apart from its closeness to the mainland, why Boa should have been chosen for this purpose.

192 *Not. Dign. Occ* xi 48 (see note 56 above). On the cemetery near the walls, with burials dated to the sixth century, see *Bull. Dalm.* 29 (1906), 3–7 and *VAHD* 45 (1922), 46 ff., where the burials are dated to the sixth and seventh centuries.

193 *PLRE* 2, 889.

194 *PLRE* 2, 708–10.

195 *PLRE* 2, 514 (Glycerius) and 777 f. (Julius Nepos). Nepos produced a coinage asserting his imperial pretensions, which circulated in Italy until his death. See J.P.C. Kent, 'Julius Nepos and the fall of the Western Empire', *Corolla Mem. E. Swoboda*

(Graz, 1966), 146–50.

196   *PLRE* 2, 815.

197   Wilkes, *Dalmatia* 423–7.

198   The latest record of an official at Salona is the proconsul Marcellinus, *CIL* III 9527, who received a letter from Pope Gregory in AD 599, *Epp.* ix, 5. The latest dated inscription is the epitaph of the Abbess Johanna who had fled from Sirmium to Salona and died there on 12th May 612: R. Egger, *Forschungen in Salona* 2 (Vienna, 1926), 109.

199   The fullest modern account of this subject is Grga Novak's *History of Split* (in Croatian *Povijest Splita*) vol. I–III (Zagreb, 1957, 1961, 1965).

200   On his life and career see Jackson, *Dalmatia* 2, 75 ff.

201   Thomas Arch. *c.* X: 'cuius domus fuerat iuxta columnas palatii supra mare'.

202   'eiectis idolis', 'proiectis', would appear to suggest removal of the sarcophagus and perhaps statues from the niches, see Bulić-Karaman, 134.

203   See Jacques Zeiller, *Les origines chrétiennes dans la province romaine de Dalmatie* (Paris, 1906); E. Dyggve, *History of Salonitan Christianity* (Oslo, 1951) and, for a summary account, Wilkes, *Dalmatia* 427 ff. The date of the Domnio's martytdom is given by an inscription of the 10th April, *CIL* III 9575 cf. Wilkes, *Dalmatia*, pl. 58, and the year is presumed to be 304, though either 303 or 305 is possible. It is doubtful whether Diocletian was in Salona at the time. His known movements exclude this for 303 and 305 and it does not appear likely that his overland journey from Ravenna to Nicomedia via the Danube in 304 (see above p. 9) would have brought him to Salona. The presence of soldiers among the martyrs, which later tradition makes members of Diocletian's bodyguard, can be explained by Salona being the residence of the provincial governor. (I am grateful to Dr George Duncan for comment on this point.)

204   For a list of Salona bishops with full discussion of sources see F. Bulić and J. Bervaldi, *Kronotaksa solinskih biskupa* (Suppl. to *Bull. Dalm.* 35, 1912, Zagreb 1912–13).

205   *Liber Pontificalis* (ed. Duchesne, 1886) vol. 1, 330. The mosaics of the Salona martyrs are illustrated in Bulić-Karaman, pl. 74; cf. R. Krautheimer, *Rome, Profile of a City, 312–1308* (Princeton, 1980), 97 f.

206   Duchesne, *MEFR* 24 (1904), 106, suggested that John of Ravenna was a fiction, being invented from Pope John X, who had been bishop of Ravenna until 914. It was he who brought order to the church in Dalmatia after the disruption caused by Croatian settlement. This was accepted by F. Bulić, cf. Bulić-Karaman, 133 f.

207   Ljubo Karaman, 'Die Anfänge des mittelälterlichen Split bis zum Jahre 800' (in Croatian with German summary), *Serta Hoffilleriana* (Zagreb, 1940), 419–36. See the approving comments of F. Dvornik, ap. Const. Porphyr. *DAI* 2, 108.

208   The column and architrave are visible in Bulić-Karaman 1929, pl. 53 and Marasović

Diocletian Palace, pl. 92.

209   Illustrated in Bulić-Karaman pl. 86 and, for its position in the Temple (Baptistery), Marasović *Diocletian Palace*, pl. 94. For a discussion of its date see Karaman *op cit*. (note 207), 427–31. In 1963 the sarcophagus of John, archbishop of Split in the tenth century, was found re-used as a tomb in the church of St Clare in the east range of the private apartments. The epitaph reveals that he was a native of Split and that his father's name was Torcadatus, the Slav Tvrtko. See B. Gabričević, *VAHD* 62, 1960 (1967), 87–103 (with French summary). For an illustration see Marasović, *Diocletian Palace*, Supplement pl. 67. It is an addition to a group of such early sarcophagi at Split: John of Ravenna (8th century), prior Peter (8th century), Queen Jelena (second half of 10th century), archbishop Martin (second half of 10th century), archbishop Laurence (second half of 11th century).

210   See F. Dvornik ap. Const. Porphyr. *DAI* 2, p. 123.

211   The chapters of Constantine Porphyrogenitus on Dalmatia and the south Slavs, *c*. 29–36, are a valuable source in a period when the historical record is at its most meagre. For a general account of the emperor (died 959) see Arnold Toynbee, *Contantine Porphyrogenitus and his World* (Oxford, 1973).

212   The evidence from excavations in 1968–74, now being published in *Split Excavations*, is surveyed by Sheila McNally, *Archaeology* 28 no. 4 (Oct. 1975), 248–59, on which the following paragraphs are based.

213   Five capitals and fragments from two sarcophagi are assigned to the 5th–6th centuries. For a late capital re-used in a post-Roman wall near the East Baths see *Split Excavations* 1, pl. 22c. What appear to have been Roman floors laid above the original Diocletian occupation were noted in the magazines near the north-east Perimeter Wall, *Split Excavations* 2, 64 f., and in the small chamber adjoining the palaestra of the East Baths, *Split Excavations* 1, 25 f. and pl. 14b, 15a.

214   *Split Excavations* 1, p 16–18 and pl. 8a–c.

215   McNally, *op. cit* (note 212) 255.

216   Bulić-Karaman, pl. 81 and for the interior of the chapel Marasović, *Diocletian Palace*, Supplement pl. 48.

217   B. Gabričević, *op cit*. (in note 209) 95

218   See Marasović, *Diocletian Palace*, pl. 22.

219   For surveys of the remains and recent restoration see *Urbs* (Split) vol. 4, 1961–62 (1965). A deposit of high-quality imported pottery of the late 14th to early 15th centuries at the north-east angle of the private apartments and close to where the external interval tower once stood has been linked with the residence of a famous figure in the history of medieval Split, Prince Hrvoje, Duke of Bosnia, Duke (Vojvod) of Split, Viceregent of Dalmatia and Croatia. In June 1413 his house near a Palace tower was sacked by the infuriated citizens of Split, and the expensive broken pottery may be the result of this. See McNally, *op. cit* (note 212) 256; Janet Buerger, *Split*

Excavations 3, 16. He had been suspected of intriguing with the Turks. He withdrew to Kotor and died in 1415. In the aftermath Split passed for good under the control of Venice. See Jackson, *Dalmatia* 2, 8 f.

220   See above p. 20 and note 71.

221   The survival of the polygonal gate towers is suggested by the possibility that the form of the gates was used by Giotto in some of his frescoes at Padua in the chapel of the Madonna dell' Arena (1303–5), notably 'The Entry into Jerusalem' and 'The Carrying of the Cross'. See John White, *Burlington Magazine* 115 (1973), no. 844, 443 ff. From the fifteenth century an illumination of a biblical scene with walls, towers and belfry of Split as a background in Hrvoje's Missal (now in Topkapi, Istanbul), commissioned by Duke Hrvoje (see above note 219), is illustrated in Marasović, *Diocletian Palace,* Supplement, pl. 2. There is also a model of the city in the hand of St Duje in the screen by G. de Santacroce (1549) in the Franciscan monastery at Poljud near Split; Marasović, *Diocletian Palace,* Supplement, pl. 3.

222   See Mommsen, *CIL* III, p. 271, on his activity in Dalmatia and, for a general account, B. Ashmole, *Proc. Brit. Acad.* 45 (1959), 25 f.

223   For a full register of these early sources, see the Serbo-Croatian edition of Bulić-Karaman, 24–43. On the round temples in the Temple precinct see above p. 55.

224   Hébrard-Zeiller, 7. They are in the collection of the Royal Institute of British Architects in London. One drawing of the Mausoleum is illustrated by Marasović, *Diocletian Palace,* Supplement pl. 4. See now the works cited by *Split Excavations* 1, 48, n. 21: Gian-Giorgio Zorzi, *I designi della antichita di Andrea Palladio* (Venice, 1959), figs. 266–7 and p. 106 and H. Spielmann, *Andrea Palladio und die Antike* (Munich-Berlin, 1966), 94–5 and 117, nos. 247–8.

225   *Voyage d'Italie, de Dalmatie, de Grèce et du Levant fait aux années 1675 et 1676,* Lyon 1678, and George Wheler, Esq., *Journey into Greece, in company of Dr. Spon of Lyons,* London 1682; also Amsterdam editions of 1689 and 1692.

226   J.B.Fischer von Erlach, *Entwurf einer historischen Architektur* (Vienna, 1721) Bk 2, X–XI. He was a leading architect to the Austrian court who designed several palaces, churches and other public buildings, including the first phase of Schönbrunn. Farlati's *Illyricum Sacrum* is a vast collection of documents in eight large volumes. See vol. I (Venice, 1751), 488–90, cap. XVI, and the reconstuction taken from Fischer von Erlach in vol. II (1753), 397.

227   Quoted from John Fleming, *Robert Adam and his Circle* (London, 1962), 237. This work offers a full account of the Dalmatian expedition based on Adam's correspondence, on which the summary given here is based.

228   Robert Adam, *Ruins of the Palace of the Emperor Diocletian at Spalato in Dalmatia* (London, 1764). The bicentenary was marked by an exhibition at Split (December 1964–January 1965), with an excellent brief catalogue by Duško Kečkemet. The protracted affair of the production of the volume is recounted by John Fleming in *The Architectural Review,* February 1958, 102–7. Clerisseau's fine drawing of the

Peristyle is illustrated by John Fleming, *op. cit.* (note 227), pl. 78.

229   Hébrard-Zeiller, 11.

230   Christopher Hibbert, *London: the Biography of a City* (Penguin ed. Harmondsworth, 1980), 120 f.

231   *Voyage pittoresque et historique d'l'Istrie et de la Dalmatie rédigé d'après l'Itinéraire de L.F Cassas par Joseph Lavallée* (Paris, 1802).

232   See his lecture, A. Hauser, *Spalato und die römische Monumente Dalmatiens* (Vienna, 1883).

233   For the increasing literature on Split up to 1927, see Bulić-Karaman (Serbo-Croatian edition), 33–43 For post-war exploration and excavation see C. Fisković, *Rad. Jug. Akad. Znanosti i uimjetnosti* 279 (Zagreb, 1950), the papers in *Urbs* 4, 1961–62 (1965) by S. Matijević and J. Matasović, and the summary in *Split Excavations* 1, 5–7.

234   *Decline and Fall of the Roman Empire,* vol. i (Everyman ed.), p. 341.

ADDENDUM 1993

The occasion of reprinting permits an attempt to correct or remove the regrettable large numbers of misprints and textual errors. The reception accorded by reviewers (N. Duval, *Bulletin Monumentale* 144 (1986), 354–6; J. Humphrey, *AJA* 91 (1987), 635; T. Marasović, *JRA* 2 (1989), 374–7; J. J. Rossiter, *Echoes du Monde classique* 31 (1987), 273–5) indicated that this little book may retain some utility for years to come. No new material has been introduced into the text but, in addition to those items cited by reviewers in discussion, a few relevant items may be noted from the register of publications relating to Split and its position in the architecture of late antiquity. The most important are the fifth and sixth volumes of *Split Excavations*, edited by Sheila McNally and others (on which see the discussion by N. Duval in *JRA* 4(1991), 378–84 and, briefly, J. J. Wilkes, *The Classical Review* xli (1991), 2,450–1). Volume V (p.3–43) contains a comprehensive discussion by Sheila McNally of the present state of knowledge regarding Split, along with a review of current controversies and an up-to-date bibliography. On more specific aspects, the connections between elements of architectural asymmetry and oblique perspectives continue to be examined in the context of late classical aesthetics, notably by G. De Angelis D'Ossat (*Palladio* n.s. 11, 3 (June 1989), 5–18. In another quarter T. Zawadzki (*Museum Helveticum* 44 (1987), 223–30 argues that in the references in the ancient sources to Split the different meanings of villa (private residence) and '*palatium*' (imperial palace) have been pressed to hard by N. Duval and his supporters. New discoveries continue to be made at Gamzirgrad in eastern Serbia, the Romulianum of the emperor Galerius (D. Srejović, *Starinar* 36 (1985), 51–67; 37(1986), 87–102. Yet as the function and character of that remarkable complex of private and public structures become more difficult to understand, the comparisons with Diocletian's villa seem less apparent.

BIBLIOGRAPHY AND ABBREVIATIONS

AE	L'Année Épigraphique. Paris, 1888 - (cited by year only).
ANRW	H. Temporini and W. Haase (eds.), *Aufstieg und Niedergang der römischen Welt*. Berlin-New York 1972-.
Arch. Iug.	*Archaeologia Iugoslavica*. Belgrade.
Barnes, *New Empire*	Timothy D. Barnes, *The New Empire of Diocletian and Constantine*. Cambridge, Mass. London, 1982.
Bulić-Karaman	Frane Bulić and Ljubo Karaman, Kaiser Diokletians Palast in Split. Zagreb, 1929. This is a shortened version, with fewer footnotes and shorter bibliographical section, of *Palaca cara Dioklecijana u Splitu*. Zagreb, 1927.
Bull Dalm	*Bulletino di archaeologia e storia dalmata*. Split. After 1927 continued as *VAHD*
CIL	*Corpus Inscriptionum Latinarum*. Berlin, 1863.
Const. Porphyr. *DAI*	Constantine Porphyrogenirus, *De Administrando Imperii*. (Vol. l) ed. Gy. Moravcsik, trans. R.J.H. Jenkins, Budapest, 1949. Also revised edition, Washington D.C., 1967. (Vol. 2) *Commentary* by F. Dvornik, R.J.H. Jenkins, B. Lewis, Gy. Moravcsik, D Obolensky, S. Runciman. Ed. R.J.H. Jenkins. London, 1962.
Duval, *Urbs*	Noël Duval, 'La place de Split dans l'architecture antique du bas-empire *Urbs* 4, 1961-62 (1965), 67-95, and in a shorter version, *Bull. Soc. Nat. Antiq. de France*, 1961, 76-117.
C. Fisković	'Prilog proučavanju i zaštiti Dioklecijanove palače u Splitu', *Rad Jugoslavenske akademije znanosti i umjetnosti* 279. Zagreb, 1950.
Hébrard-Zeiller	E. Hébrard and J. Zeiller, *Spalato, le Palais de Diocletien*. Paris, 1912.
ILS	*Inscriptiones Latinae Selectae*, ed. H. Dessau. Berlin, 1892-1916.
Jackson, *Dalmatia*	T.G. Jackson, *Dalmatia, The Qvarnero and Istria*. 3 vols. Oxford, 1883.
Lactantius, *De Mort. Pers.*	Lactantius, *De Mortibus Persecutorum*. Edited and translated by J.L. Creed. Oxford, 1984.

Marasović, *Diocletian Palace*	Jerko and Tomislav Marasović, *Diocletian Palace*. Zagreb, 1970. (See also T. Marasović, *Diocletian's Palace*, Belgrade, 1982 with several new illustrations.)
Marasović, *Urbs*	J. and T. Marasović, 'A survey of exploration, preservation and restoration work carried out in the Palace of Diocletian between 1955 and 1965', *Urbs* (Split) 4, 1961-62 (196S), 23-54 and 149-152 (English summary).
McNally, Sheila	'Ausgrabungen im Diokletianspalast zu Split', *Antike Welt* 10, 1979, Hft. 2, 35-46
MEFR(A)	*Mélanges d'Archéologie et d'Histoire de l'École Française de Rome* (after 1970 split into series *Antiquite and Moyen Age*). Paris.
Niemann	G. Niemann, *Der Palast Diokletians in Spalato*. Vienna 1910.
PBSR	*Papers of the British School at Rome*. Rome.
PECS	*The Princeton Encyclopedia of Classical Sites* ed. R. Stillwell, W L. MacDonald and M H. McAllister. Princeton, 1976.
PLRE	*The Prosopography of the Later Roman Empire. Vol. 1: AD 260 395* . (A.H.M. Jones, J.R. Martindale and J. Morris). Cambridge, 1971. *Vol 2: AD 395 527*. (J.R. Martindale). Cambridge, 1980.
Popescu, *Inscripţiile*	Em. Popescu, *Inscripţiile Greceşti şi Latine din secolele IV–XIII descoperite în România*. Bucharest, 1976.
RE	*Realencyclopädie der classichen Altertumswissenschaft,* ed. Pauly, Wissowa, etc. Stuttgart, 1893-.
Split Excavations	*Diocletian's Palace: Joint Excavations in Southeast Quarter,* Pt. 1, J. and T. Marasović, S. McNally, and J. Wilkes. Split, 1972. *Diocletian's Palace: American-Yugoslav Joint Excavations. Pt. 2,* S. McNally, J. and T. Marasović. Split, 1976. Pt. 3, ed. S. McNally, J. and T. Marasović: Janet Buerger: The Medieval Glazed Pottery. Mary R. DeMaine: The Medieval Glass. Claudia Smith: The Roman Mosaics. Split, 1979.
Strzygowski, *Markstein*	J. Strzygowski, 'Spalato, ein Markstein der römanischen Kunst bei ihrem Übergänge, vom Orient nach dem Abendlande', *Studien aus Kunst*

	und Geschichte Fr. Schneider gewidmet. Fribourg in Breisgau, 1906, 325-336 = *Bull. Dalm. XXXI* (1908) Suppl. I (Ital. trans.), and in French by Duval, *Bull Soc Nat Antiq. de France,* 1961, 110-17.
Thomas Arch.	Thomas Archidiaconus, *Histonria Salonitana.* Ed. F. Racki, *Monumenta Spectanta historiam slavorum meridionalium xxvi.* Zagreb, 1894.
Wilkes, *Dalmatia*	J.J. Wilkes, *Dalmatia (History of the Roman Provinces).* London, 1969.
Williams, *Diocletian*	Stephen Williams, *Diocletian and the Roman Recovery.* London, 1985.
VAMZ	*Vijesnik Arheološkog muzeja u Zagrebu,* Zagreb.
VAHD	*Vijesnik za Arheologiju i Historiju Dalmatinsku,* (supersedes *Bull. Dalm.* from 1927). Split.